D1139006

SILENT
MIND
GOLF

ALSO BY ROBIN SIEGER

BOOKS
Natural Born Winners
You Can Change Your Life Anytime You Want
42 Days to Wealth, Health and Happiness
Passport to Success

AUDIO
Natural Born Winners
Pathway to Peace of Mind
Pathway To Success
NBW Guided Meditation

SILENT
MIND
GOLF

How to Empty Your Mind
and Play Golf Instinctively

ROBIN SIEGER

FOREWORD BY TONY JACKLIN

First published in Great Britain
2010 by Aurum Press Ltd
7 Greenland Street
London NW1 0ND
www.aurumpress.co.uk

A catalogue record for this book is available from the British Library.

ISBN 978 1 84513 548 5

3 5 7 9 10 8 6 4 2
2010 2012 2014 2013 2011

Original text design by George Triay, www.triaydesign.com
Adapted and typeset by Saxon Graphics Ltd, Derby
Printed in China

To
The Fabulous Molly Kershaw

CONTENTS

FOREWORD

I wish I'd had this book over 30 years ago — I genuinely believe it would have prolonged my career at the highest level. There was nothing like this in the game, and yet all of us acknowledged even then how important the mind is in playing this great game of ours. Through the years the greatest golfers have had the strongest minds — Hogan, Snead, Nicklaus, Woods. It's their mental mastery that has set them apart.

To play our best golf we need to stop listening to the inner voice of self-doubt that plagues every golfer, and be in control. Many, many books have been written about the theories of the mind, but at last here is one that shows you how to make your mind work *for* you and *with* you. It's simple and effective, and I believe it works.

Robin not only understands the game, he also has a great passion for it. This comes through when you spend time with him and it comes through in his book. The first person I gave a copy to was my son — he already has a great golf swing, but nowadays that's not enough. I hope this helps him enjoy the game of golf as much as I have.

Tony Jacklin
Florida

INTRODUCTION

GETTING TO THAT 'EUREKA!' MOMENT

My father Albert was at one time a scratch golfer. I remember as a small boy going with him on a Saturday or Sunday afternoon to Erskine Golf Club, where he would take his clubs to the practice ground and hit balls hour after hour. I didn't understand what he was doing, other than having fun hitting balls. I later realised that this dedication to practice is an essential part of greatness in golf. In fact, **greatness in any endeavour is the result of dedicated practice**.

Throughout his life, my father would practise on a regular basis and his handicap was never worse than five. I, on the other hand, rarely practised and would invest in technology and books in my pursuit of shortcuts to the perfect game, which I naturally felt would save me time on the practice range and shots on the course. The truth is that I found practice boring. I typically hit such a variety of wayward shots that I became convinced the solution to my problem was technical, and so I changed my swing on a regular basis. Sometimes it would be my grip, other times my stance. For a while the plane of my swing was too flat, then too upright. My tempo was too fast or too slow, my stance was too open or too closed. In short, there was such a multitude of things that I felt were wrong, and could go wrong, with my swing at any time that all my efforts at practice were, I believed, simply reinforcing bad habits. Those excuses supported my inclination to be lazy when it came to practice. Clearly, I showed no signs of inheriting the sense of dedication that my father had displayed for so many years.

While an undergraduate at the University of Surrey in the 1970s, I played for the university golf team. Before you get too excited about my abilities, I think it's only fair to say that the standard was not that high. In fact, owning a set of golf clubs, understanding etiquette and being able to break 85 would generally guarantee you a place on the team. Even though I didn't have an official handicap when I went to university (or at least one that I was willing to admit to!), I was keen to be accepted by the University Golf Society and to gain student membership at one of the local courses. I told the captain that my handicap had lapsed the previous year; I had a handicap at the time of around 14. I just thought that as a Scotsman at an English university I should try to retain an air of mystique and allow them to assess my talent for what it was, and I hoped not to betray the game my countrymen claim to have invented.

The team trial was played at West Hill Golf Club in Surrey. At the time, my golf clubs were an eclectic mix at best – I possessed no woods, a set of 20-year-old irons, an even older pitching-wedge and a putter of unknown origins. In truth, though I enjoyed it, I did not play golf a great deal.

So, armed with a near vintage set of irons and a handicap circa 14, I arrived at the first tee, to be informed we would be playing off the back tees as the university team wished to replicate competition conditions. I have few memories of that round, other than that I was driving off the tee with a three-iron and managed to hit it a very long way (for a three-iron). This was in part due to the fact that I had to create a swing that would enable me to launch the ball further off the tee than normal. The only drawback was that the new swing I had created was of little use to me on the fairway.

I shot a 77, eight over par, and was promptly welcomed into the University of Surrey golf team. Through all the years that followed I had one or two rounds under 80 – the majority of my golf continued to be played to a handicap of around 14. As I got older and was able to afford better equipment, I invested in new clubs, thinking it was a possible solution. I also had a couple of lessons, yet, try as I might, I was unable to improve my game. Obviously I hadn't yet realised the need to dedicate time and effort to practice or mental preparation. I was, I imagine, still looking for a short cut, the magic bullet, a miracle, or some lucky charm that would save me all the bother of dedicated practice.

I continued to play golf socially after I left university, and indeed entered a number of competitions. I generally played well enough and had some good wins, both in stroke play and match play, but I never really improved as a player. Eventually my handicap settled at around 12. Sometimes I would play a little better than that, but more often than not, much, much worse. I stopped reading the instruction guides in magazines and taking tips from well-intentioned friends, and I accepted and believed that I was a bit of a hacker whose game was never going to significantly improve.

In my career over the last 20 years I have specialised in the psychology of peak performance and success. I have worked with organisations and individuals to identify specifically the qualities that enabled them to stand out from the rest of their field. I help my clients save their best performance for when it matters and to succeed again and again.

I have written a number of books (including an international bestseller, *Natural Born Winners*) examining what truly lies at the heart of greatness in sport, business and, most importantly of all, life. Time and time again I have reached the unerring conclusion that our ability to be successful is not found in the way we work, it is found in the way that we think. The way we think influences the way we behave and the way we perceive the world around us. I have seen that truth manifested in many different business sectors and sporting fields. However, I had never really believed that anyone could, in an instant and at will, change their golfing ability simply by adopting a positive attitude. That would be far too simplistic for a game as complex as golf.

Something unexpected happened to me in 2007 that would not just challenge that notion, but blow it out of the water forever. I had a very simple idea about improving performance on the golf course. In fact it would not be inaccurate to call it a 'Eureka!' moment. It came when I decided to apply my work-related techniques to my own game of golf – by this time I was only managing to play eight to ten rounds a year.

I had recently joined Nairn Golf Club in Scotland. It is a wonderful championship course where they played the Walker Cup in 1999. Without a handicap I was unable to enter any competitions, or play matches with other members, so I had to get a handicap. The secretary told me to submit three cards and play off the back tees and, based on these scores, I would be given an official handicap.

The next day I asked my friend Shaun if he would play with me and sign my card. I had already decided to employ my earlier 'Eureka!' theory and approach this, and all future rounds, by applying a new thought process to my game. I then proceeded to play one of the best rounds of my life. The next day I went out for a second round – and played even better than I had the day before. Two weeks later I played a third round and was given my official playing handicap of eight.

In those two weeks I discovered that previously I had been concentrating all my efforts on technique and mechanics, and that I had given no thought at all to the origins of performance excellence. I now realise there are two significant sources to performance excellence. My father was the first source of enlightenment (although it took me some time to figure that out). He was a role model through his dedication to the game and his commitment to practice. I came to understand the second source of performance excellence through a combination of my own mental struggles with the game and the success I saw with my clients. This second element – the reality of how mental conditioning techniques can successfully be applied to the game of golf – forms the subject of this book.

I will not claim to be qualified to guide you through the mechanics of the golf swing. I am, however, in a unique position to explain how the psychology of success can be applied to the mental preparation required for peak performance in golf.

SILENT
MIND

.

SILENT MIND

I decided to call my new approach to the mental conditioning aspect of golf *Silent Mind*. This most accurately describes what happens when I play my best golf: I play with no thoughts (positive or negative), no internal mental chatter, no anxiety over the possibility of a bad outcome, no memories of previous bad shots in similar situations. I have trained my mind to be completely and utterly still, as though I am in a meditative state. I play with a silent mind.

Over the past 25 years I have studied and researched a great deal of 'success' literature, and though the language used and examples may differ, the fundamentals that lie at the heart of success remain the same. If I were to give a young person the basic rules of success based on what I have learned, I would say, 'Know what you want, plan how to get it, and believe you can succeed.' I would even add that, initially, they need not worry too much about the specifics. I would reinforce the importance of self-belief, commitment and learning from failure. But, critically, **it is important to avoid identifying with failure**, as so many do. This is precisely what I had been doing on the golf course for 35 years, until I teed up at Nairn Golf Club in Scotland in 2007.

THE THREE KEYS IN THE *SILENT MIND*
APPROACH TO GOLF

FOCUS

Just as an archer needs a target to aim at before firing an arrow, so too do we, as golfers, need a precise target of where we want the ball to finish. Most people *think* they have a target they are aiming at. Usually it is vague – it will be an area of the fairway or the green where they hope the ball will finish up. If you have a vague target you will have a vague outcome. **Focus** in the *Silent Mind* means that you must identify exactly where you want the ball to finish. This is critically important, and must be understood and applied. **You need a *precise* spot on the fairway or the green where you want the ball to finish.** It must be a realistic target, and it must be achievable under normal circumstances. I mention this now because people have asked me why do I not focus on holing every shot from the fairway. The answer is because it is not realistic, and therefore the subconscious mind will reject it as being possible. The focus must be on an outcome that our brain can a) lock onto and b) process as being realistic and achievable. **We *must* give the subconscious mind a target to lock onto, so we focus on the exact outcome of each and every shot.**

FAITH

Faith is the ability to believe something based on trust. I have come to understand that, before I hit a shot, irrespective of what I might tell myself, **if I do not have the faith in my ability to execute the shot, it is very unlikely to happen.** The reason is that, at a subconscious level, self-doubt will interfere with the natural execution of the muscle memory sequence. We all know of players, from top professionals to weekend warriors, who have choked in competition when the pressure became too great – often, I believe, because they lost faith in themselves. **The slightest self-doubt is all it takes to start the collapse**. I, too, have choked on many occasions in competition or even during a fun round when I was playing very well, because, at a critical point, I stopped believing that I could hit the important shots because I started to doubt myself.

I have often noted that young, pre-school children appear to have remarkably high self-esteem. They are confident in themselves and believe that they can do anything they put their mind to. Their self-image is positive and complete. It is sad to reflect that, in most cases, by the time children have grown older and entered adolescence few still have such high self-esteem. Why? It's because, due to a multitude of external factors over which they have had no control (parental, educational and peer group negative inputs), they have lost their internal positive self-image, their faith in themselves and their ability to succeed.

On the golf course, as in many other areas of life, we need a childlike faith in ourselves. We need to believe that we are capable of achieving what we have set out to achieve. There is no place for self-doubt on the golf course; just as there is no place for self-doubt in life as we seek to create our own victories.

PRESENCE

In the *Silent Mind* it is important that you have no thoughts in your mind when you are about to play the shot. You must be wholly in the present moment. Just before an important putt, drive or wedge shot, how often have you remembered a similar shot that went badly? How often, when faced with out-of-bounds up the right side of the fairway, have you said to yourself, 'Don't slice it'? And, as you've said it, you have already visualised this precise future outcome (the focus point in your subconscious mind, mentioned earlier) that you do not want to occur.

The capacity to be _in the moment_ allows us to play with freedom. I have read many accounts of people who were leading major tournaments confess to getting ahead of themselves and thinking about the things that could go wrong over the remaining holes, or even what they were going to say during their acceptance speech. In so doing, their attention was taken away from the present moment, the here and now. It is worth reflecting that **the future does not exist; it is by our actions in the present moment that we determine future outcomes.** Which is why, within the game of golf, we need to be _present in the moment_, unencumbered by thought.

If you think of your brain as a computer, what software would you want to install? Would you want to load cheap, untested, badly duplicated software? Or would you want the very best, state-of-the-art, technologically superior software? I would like you to think of the _Silent Mind_ system as superior software for your golfing brain.

Unfortunately your brain does not come with a disc that you can install. _Silent Mind_ is a process you have to learn. Once practised and applied, you will see results quickly. On more than one occasion I have outlined the basics of the method to a person on a golf course and seen an immediate improvement in their game, there and then – sometimes with quite spectacular results. But a note of caution: like all things in life, without regular practice, the system's effectiveness will be diluted.

> **'I never became a good player until I got out of thinking too many details and learned to focus.'**
>
> Ben Hogan

SHOOTING HOOPS

I was told of an experiment conducted in America many years ago by a psychology professor working with university basketball players. The professor decided to measure the ability of the players, with the goal of improving their penalty-throwing (free throws) statistics. He split the players into three groups of 10. The first group he asked to practise for two hours a week instead of one. The second group he asked to practise with more concentration but only for an hour. The third group he asked not to practise at all but simply to sit and imagine they were throwing perfect shots every time. After one month they went back and had a penalty-throwing competition. The group who had been practising for two hours instead of one showed no improvement, the group that practised for one hour but with more concentration showed a slight improvement. However, the group who had not practised at all but had simply visualised throwing the penalty shots in a perfect manner had improved noticeably.

I have no doubt that you will be familiar with the notion of positive psychology and the power of positive thinking. I am sure you also understand the benefits of having a positive mental attitude on the golf course. You may even have read about visualising the shot and staying calm on the course. These techniques are all important. However, I doubt any of you have ever, on a daily basis, spent ten to fifteen minutes actually visualising yourself hitting perfect shots. Seeing yourself, as if through a camera lens, from a number of different angles, with a perfect swing. Feeling the emotion that the perfect shot can bring.

To maximise our potential as golfers it is important we understand that **the more time and effort we put into the game off the course, in developing our mental powers of focus and mindfulness, the more significantly we will improve our actual playing experience.** This is time not only well spent, but time which will, I believe, for the average golfer, deliver the greatest improvement in the shortest span.

I have noticed that, for many recreational golfers, the first game they play after a long winter lay-off is often their best round of the year. They will tell me that they had just gone out for a casual warm-up game – to blow away the winter cobwebs. They had no expectations of playing well and were often not even keeping score. In effect they were approaching the game with no thoughts (positive or negative). Because they had not played for a few months, their expectations were low, they were not worrying about the outcome of the shots, the game was of no significance, and therefore they were swinging the club with very little thought at all.

Without realising it, they have partially attained the *Silent Mind* state. They are not consciously thinking about shaping the ball or where the ball is going to land.

Unfortunately, almost without exception, as soon as we start to play well the conscious mind kicks in and thinks to itself, 'I need to take charge' – which is exactly the opposite of what needs to happen.

CATCH IT!

Have you ever caught something that was falling off a table, such as a knife, a fork or even a glass? You reacted instinctively, and in the process averted what could have been an embarrassing or dangerous outcome. In these situations something happens so suddenly that we have to react before we think. Our subconscious mind takes over and coordinates all the movements and actions – in a very precise sequence – that need to occur if we're to catch the falling object. Quite simply, we do not have the time to think, and so we just don't.

In golf we have all the time in the world to think before a shot, and ironically, rather than a benefit, I believe for the majority of golfers this is a handicap. When faced with a difficult shot, how often do we start to think negatively? How often do we imagine missing the putt, or hooking the tee shot out of bounds or slicing it into the lake? How often have we walked up to a delicate chip over a bunker and had a full 90 seconds to worry about it before we arrive at the ball? We then take far more practice swings than we normally would – all the time, the mind is worrying about the consequences of a bad shot, and this somehow manages to overwhelm any positive thoughts we are trying to embed in our minds.

While standing in the practice area by the chipping green we throw soft lob after soft lob from a variety of lies unerringly onto the practice green. Yet, when out on the course in the competition or during a match, and faced with a shot we may have practised 20 times only an hour earlier, we stop trusting our swing and try to control it very deliberately. *We are thinking too much*. The left side of the brain is trying to control the swing; the right side of the brain is trying to control our emotions. Something has to give, and usually that will be the swing.

Let's go back to the moment you caught the falling glass. You simply reacted to a situation that was unfolding in front of you. You were not thinking, you were purely doing. I would like to give you an exercise to demonstrate this principle.

CATCH ►

This exercise is not about catching a ball; it is about trusting your motor skills and subconscious mind.

Get a tennis ball or a small beanbag that you can throw and catch easily with one hand. Then get a partner to stand eight to twelve feet away from you. I want you to throw the ball to each other very gently and catch it with one hand. Do this for about one minute, or ten throws each.

After you have finished the first part of this exercise I want you to throw the ball again to each other. The difference this time is that you must maintain full eye contact with your partner. I do not want you to watch the ball at all. I want you to focus entirely on the eyes of the person who is throwing the ball. Do not under any circumstances follow the ball in the air. The ball will be in your peripheral vision throughout the exercise and you will trust your brain to make the calculations that are required to catch it.

Once you have done this for a minute or so I want you to alternate the hand with which you catch and throw the ball, all the time maintaining eye contact with your partner. Continue this exercise for another two to three minutes, until you become very comfortable with the idea of not following the ball. Rather, maintain eye contact with the other person without any worry whatsoever about dropping the ball. It is probable that while doing this you will drop the ball a number of times. But remember: this exercise is not about catching, it is about trusting your instinctive actions.

THE JUGGLER

Have you ever watched a juggler and wondered how they are able to process so much complex information and perform with an effortless ease that holds you spellbound? When you think logically, it is extraordinarily complex. Each ball is sent on a journey, which is mathematically predictable in terms of speed, trajectory and the position in space where the juggler has to intercept it. Then the ball is sent back on a very similar but not identical path, so that when it returns it is never to exactly the same place. The throwing and catching pattern is continually changing.

Masters of the juggling art perform feats that defy belief, yet the basic pattern of juggling three balls is something almost anyone can learn through dedicated practice (usually after about 20 to 30 minutes of trying). Like the catching exercise, it is a result of instinctive reactions. Is it such a leap of faith, then, to believe that the golf swing we have been practising and refining all these years probably works sufficiently well to enable us to hit the shots we wish to without too much conscious intervention?

Every professional juggler is using the same technique to juggle as every other juggler, yet we have no trouble recognising that they are all different. One only has to watch professional golfers in any tournament to see a huge variety of swings, some long, some short, some very upright, some flat, some with much body movement and some with very little. Just as each juggler has a unique style of juggling, or every one of us has a unique style of handwriting, so each golfer has a unique swing. Many swings have the look and feel of what is considered to be perfection: Ben Hogan, Ernie Els, Tony Lema, Tom Weiskopf and Tiger Woods all have near-perfect swings – and, between them, many major trophies. There are other players who have very idiosyncratic swings, swings that no one copies because they are just too unusual. Nevertheless, when we look at these players' swings, they have one thing in common – they are all doing the basics right.

The ball has no idea of the juggler's technique. Its flight path is determined by the force and direction in which it is released. The golf ball, too, can only reflect what happens to it at the moment of contact with the club-head.

So, as long as we are doing the basics right, chances are we should be able to deliver the club-head to the ball and in turn effect the outcome we desire. I encourage everyone who takes up golf to get lessons on the basics of the swing. For me the basics are *stance*, *grip*, *balance* and *tempo*. If you understand the impact that the basics have on your capacity to make a good swing, then you can, in effect, create your own unique swing with the knowledge that it will do the job.

LEARN FROM THE CHILD

Have you ever seen a child on a putting green for the first time? Normally a parent gives him, or her, a cut-down club and a few balls. After a few attempts to hit the ball he quickly gets the hang of what is expected: knocking the ball in the hole – what could be simpler?

The child hasn't had lessons – he doesn't understand the importance of grip, balance and tempo. He looks at the ball, then looks at the hole, and then, more often than not, starts to swing away and soon sinks a few putts. He has no notion of complexity nor worry or anxiety about the outcome. I have no doubt the child wants to sink the putt, but equally he doesn't seem to be unduly upset if he misses, as he is just happy with the experience of being out there hitting the ball. It is this ability to be relaxed, with no preconceived notions of how he should be swinging the club, that enables the child – often trying for the first time – to start sinking putts. Without realising it, he has focused on the target (the hole), and he has no memory of past 'bad' shots or worries about a missed putt. So again, without realising it, he is in the moment – doing unwittingly the one thing we have forgotten: to be entirely focused on the present. **We have forgotten to not worry about the outcome and just swing the club.**

NEGATIVE SELF-THOUGHT

When we face a difficult or important shot in golf – anything from a 235-yard fairway wood to an island green surrounded by water or a 16-inch downhill putt to win the match – we rarely approach the shot in a completely calm and relaxed manner. As much as we would all like to be Zen monks in a state of total calm, somehow or other we get ahead of ourselves. **When a shot is high-risk and high-reward, we tend to focus on the risk**. This usually takes the form of negative self-thoughts, and we find ourselves saying, 'Whatever you do, don't hit it in the water,' or, 'If I miss this putt, I'll lose the game.' Even if we say something positive like, 'Make a good swing, keep your head down, finish the swing, nice tempo,' more often than not we believe the negative thought, because it has a higher emotional value. Therefore, **understand that any negative self-thought or self-doubt is going to impact on the shot you are about to play**.

In sport, people often talk about being 'in the zone'. When a sports person enters the elusive 'zone', there is only a sense of certainty. They describe a feeling where time stands still, and they truly believe that they can do anything they imagine. They are so focused on what they are going to do that they are acting unconsciously in the present moment. Nothing *mental* is getting in the way of their *physically* playing the best shot they are capable of. There are no negative thoughts – or positive thoughts. **Even a positive thought is a distraction to the mind**. In fact, there are no thoughts at all.

I can think of only a very few occasions in my life playing golf when I too found myself playing at a level at which I had never played before (or 'in the zone'). On those occasions the game became almost ridiculously easy, and there was a sense of knowing – just *knowing*, with complete faith and certainty – that every shot I hit was going to be fine. These moments have been few and far between, and though some have occurred when playing by myself, there have been others which occurred in the heat of battle, coming down the last few holes in an important match. Every time, my game has been transformed.

> **'When I get it going it's like I am in a trance. I know what's going on around me but I can black out everything. It's like I'm hypnotised. I can see the things that are going to happen. I feel like I am going to birdie every hole.'**
>
> Johnny Miller, explaining his brilliant form at the US Open in 1975

DOMINANT THOUGHT

What is *your* dominant thought when you're playing golf? When I have asked other golfers the same question, they look at me somewhat puzzled. For many years my dominant thoughts were negative. On the first tee I sometimes convinced myself that I would somehow manage to lose the match, or, if I was scoring well in a stroke-play event, that I would eventually blow up. And, surprise, surprise, I almost always did. I never imagined that I was clairvoyant or psychic; I later discovered that *my thoughts* were the architects of my self-fulfilling prophecy.

The mind is an amazingly sophisticated piece of engineering but it is also extremely simple to operate. To return to the metaphor of a computer, your PC is a very complex machine, but it can only do what its software allows it to do. And the same is true of the brain. If you think of your dominant thought as a piece of software which influences your expectations, and if you understand that your subconscious mind is trying to align your expectations with your dominant thought, you will see why negative thoughts create this self-sabotage mechanism.

If, on the first tee, you believe that you will probably lose the match by making some silly mistake at a critical point, then once out on the golf course your subconscious mind will maintain this image (which you created and input) as its dominant thought; it will do everything in its power to make this thought a reality. How often in your golfing life have you been on the course and shouted out in exasperation after hitting a spectacularly bad shot – a shank, a double hit, a thin, a slice, a hook (the list goes on and on) – 'I knew I was going to do that'? We've all done it.

This is why it is important that your dominant thought is positive. You need to *believe* you are going to win, to *believe* you are going to play well. Believing you will win and play well does not guarantee you will break the course record, but it does significantly increase your chances of playing better. Conversely, **believing you will lose or play badly almost guarantees that you will do just that**.

Silent Mind golf demands that: **prior to playing, all our thoughts are positive; and, while actually playing the shot, we have no thoughts at all – we *silence* the mind.**

We will go on to look at how you can eliminate negative thoughts – because, just like rabbits, negative thoughts very quickly multiply and spread to all areas of your thinking.

Bill Shankly, who as manager of Liverpool football club became one of English football's most famous and successful coaches, once claimed, 'Football is not a matter of life and death, it's much more important than that.' It's a wonderful quote because it allows us to understand the depth of emotion and importance sport can play in the lives of those who compete, watch or manage. But, irrespective of what Shankly and other legendary managers, players and prize-winning sports writers have said, sport, in the final analysis, is just a game to be played. Certainly the rewards can be high and intoxicating, and the penalties of failure heartbreaking and painful to accept. But, as clichéd as it may sound, it is just a game, and as far as I can remember – way back to my childhood – games are to be played because they are fun, and because we enjoy them. At the highest levels of the PGA tournaments, it is the players who are smiling and appear to be enjoying themselves who I always look for and enjoy watching.

Enjoying the game is not just about having fun; it also helps in the pursuit of excellence. **By making a conscious effort to relax and enjoy ourselves, we assist the mind in becoming quiet**. By enabling the mind to relax, we put ourselves in the perfect state to enter *Silent Mind*.

> ## 'Thinking instead of acting is the number-one golf disease.'
> Sam Snead

BELIEVE IN YOUR SWING

I doubt very much that the average golfer truly trusts their swing at all. I imagine they swing more in hope than in confidence. We frequently read about professionals who endeavoured to build a swing that will stand up under the greatest pressure. I remember a quotation by Ray Floyd that really captured the essence of pressure on the swing.

He said, 'Every golfer on the PGA Tour has two swings: one to use all year round, and the other they save for the last five holes of a major when they are in the lead.'

If you do not trust someone you employ to do a good job, you will continually be checking on them and watching to make sure they are doing what they are employed to do. If you do not trust your partner on the golf course to make the right decision, then you will automatically be watching them and offering advice that is probably unwelcome. **If you do not trust your swing, you will be tinkering with it and trying to change it right up until the point of impact with the ball.**

No one has the perfect swing. Even those swings which have been singled out because of their perfection would reveal flaws when put under a microscope. The swing you have developed at this point in your life is not perfect; it may vary from excellent to diabolically bad in the eyes of professional instructors. But **the game of golf is not scored according to the aesthetic beauty of the swing or by the metronomic tempo with which we strike the ball; it is only measured by the player who took the least number of shots**.

You have to believe in your swing. If you don't, you will remain where you are in terms of ability and never see any major improvement because deep down your belief will be, 'My swing is terrible.'

Of course there are fundamental elements of the golf swing, without which you will never be able to create consistent repetition and the correct **muscle memory** to hit the ball reliably. As I have already been at pains to point out, for people taking up the game of golf, it is essential that they learn the fundamentals of the game, if possible from a professional instructor. Whether you have been playing for five months or 30 years, if you are looking to make a significant improvement in your game, you need to make sure that the basics of the swing are present.

Once you have those basics in place and have spent time practising on a regular basis, thereby embedding muscle memory, you will be ready to start your mental conditioning practice. You will no longer swing the club in the hope that the shot will be okay. Rather, you will swing with confidence and the knowledge that your swing can be trusted. **Believing in yourself – and your swing – is the foundation of both life and golfing success.**

MUSCLE MEMORY

I've read that physiologists estimate that the basic squat, an exercise where you stand with your feet apart and then lower your body at the knee then raise it back up again to the standing position, involves the use of 256 muscles. If that simple exercise requires a sequence of motion involving 256 muscles, some to provide power and others to provide balance, how much more complex must the sequence of muscle memory be for executing a good golf swing?

The complexity of the golf swing should not be underestimated, but equally neither should it be seen as a puzzle to be cracked or a mystery to be solved. I prefer to think of all complicated muscle memory as a flow of sequences (including muscle constriction, extension and balance) that can be executed with effortless, unthinking precision. However, before reaching this state of flow, we need to have a sequence to memorise. Once learnt, each of us naturally introduces our own changes to make it work best for us. Similarly, we were all taught the same system of writing at primary school, yet within 10 years we all developed unique handwriting styles. Years later we retain the same proper grammar, alphabet and sequence, but we do not consciously think of how the words appear aesthetically on the paper.

The squat is pure muscle memory. Because we have no concern as to the outcome of the squat, we don't override the muscle memory.

When we remove all thoughts of past and future outcomes from our mind, we allow it to be at its most effective in terms of automatic muscle memory.

The purpose of practising our golf swing is to groove muscle memory into our subconscious mind, so that when we are out on the course we can let go of the need to consciously control (or think about) our swing – so that we can swing a club with no more thought than we would when doing a squat.

EMOTIONAL ENGAGEMENT

When we stand over a shot, chances are we feel either positive or negative. Very rarely are we completely neutral – detached from any emotional significance attributable to the shot. When under pressure, or when the outcome of the shot is crucial, some people have the capacity to tune out negative thoughts, visualise what they want to happen and hit the shot they need. The average golfer, from my experience, is not like that. Usually they will entertain the bad outcome. They will try to hit it too hard, or will think about losing the game. They do not dwell on these thoughts; very few of us ever do. I am sure we simply acknowledge them for a moment prior to hitting the shot, but that involuntary thought is all it takes to trigger an emotional response which generally manifests itself through a degree of tension, such as feeling 'butterflies in the tummy' or, in extreme cases, mild panic.

I have heard professional golfers speak of nerves so bad that they physically shook – or thought they were going to throw up on the first tee. These are extreme examples that few of us are likely to encounter in our club monthly medal. But the experience is the same for us as we look at the shot we absolutely have to hit well. **Even a momentary negative thought will make us tense up**. It may cause us to dwell on previous bad outcomes. Fatally, it has engaged our thinking mind, and will distract us when what we really need to do is switch off from conscious thought and allow the muscle memory to do the rest.

About 10 years ago I went to visit a friend in Sydney, Australia. After the long flight I came down with flu, so for a few days I was laid low. After four days my friend's wife told me about Long Reef Golf Club, an excellent public golf course nearby where I could get a tee-time to play.

I went down to the course that afternoon to make a tee-time for the following day. There was also an American retiree looking for a starting time. We were told they were very busy the next day, but if we were willing to tee just before seven in the morning we could have that time. We agreed to play the next morning. I turned up with a set of golf clubs borrowed from my friend's brother; I was wearing some running shoes as I had not brought any golfing shoes with me, and bought a sleeve of three balls from the pro shop.

The American, Steve, was in his mid-sixties. He had been a scratch golfer earlier in life and now played off a handicap of four – I was impressed. I remember thinking with some dismay that I had not played for a few months, was getting over flu, had borrowed clubs, was wearing a pair of training shoes, was tired and was playing an unfamiliar course in hot weather that was only going to get hotter.

By way of an early apology I told Steve that I had played at college but not very seriously since then. I was making an excuse before we even began play to justify the terrible shots that, I felt sure, were awaiting me on the course. I also remember telling myself to relax and have fun: to not worry at all about the outcome of the shots and just have a good morning on the course. Which was exactly what I did, from the minute my first tee shot landed on the middle of the fairway until I walked off the sixth green three under par. Steve was cracking jokes about my play, questioning the authenticity of my claims on the first tee. I remember saying to him that I had never been under par after nine holes and things were looking good today.

The next hole was a long par-five with the out-of-bounds down the left. I can still hear the internal voice as I stood at the seventh tee: 'Whatever you do, do not hook it out of bounds.' I then imagined the very shot I did not want to play – and immediately tensed up. Suddenly three under par with three holes to go seemed like a mountain to climb. I burst the bubble of confidence and positive self-belief.

I did not hook the ball out of bounds. In fact, I express-mailed it right into grass so deep that I immediately knew I had to play a provisional, which I did. I finished the hole two over par. Steve, fully aware of my choke, kindly distracted me by starting a conversation about barbershop quartets (it is amazing the detail of memory when under stress or heightened emotional states), and somehow I was able to let the bad shot go. The next two holes I played in a very concentrated manner. I was not relaxed, and I was not thinking positively, but somehow I managed to hole two very good putts on the eighth and ninth greens to finish the front half one under par.

It is interesting to note that while I was relaxed and had no expectations of the game ahead, my emotions were in the neutral position; I didn't care – win, lose or draw. However, once I started playing well, I became emotionally connected with negative thoughts of keeping my ball out of bounds.

If we understand the impact negative emotions can have on our swing flow, and continue to allow ourselves to think negatively, this will continue to inhibit us at critical moments of the game and leave us feeling there is nothing we can do about it. This will spoil our enjoyment of the game and prevent us from making progress. However, the good news is that, by learning to switch off our thought process, we will also switch off any negative expectations and their associated destructive emotions.

FOCUS

FOCUS

The first aspect of *Silent Mind* which we need to understand and engage is **focus**. Focus is when we look at a physical situation – the hole we are playing – and then determine in our mind's eye our target – where we want the ball to finish. That's it. **We simply focus on where we want the ball to end up**. **We do not think about or imagine all the places we *do not* want the ball to go**. So when we step up to the shot we look at the position – the exact place – on the fairway we want to play the next shot from. Obviously we will be *aware* of all the surroundings: the water hazards, the bunkers, and any other areas we do not want to visit. However, we will not pay any *attention* to them – we will not think about the ball going there.

Even though this sounds very obvious and indeed simple, I am amazed how often people 'see' the negative. They invest their attention in the stronger emotional outcome, which is pain not pleasure. This means that **people tell themselves, 'Don't go in the rough. Don't hit it out of bounds' – then do exactly that!** This is very frustrating and results in us feeling inadequate as golfers and seeing ourselves as less capable than we truly are.

The brain processes information. It doesn't assign value to it, it just assigns an outcome. If we put in the wrong information, such as the possibility of hooking into a bunker, the brain will process that, with no interpretation of whether the imagined outcome is good or bad. When we focus our attention on not hooking into the bunker, our brain simply locks onto that as the intended outcome. Which is why people who have been lifelong slicers of the ball can suddenly, to their amazement, produce a hook out of nowhere. So we need to avoid putting the possibility of a mistake into our brain in the first place.

This ability to focus is evident among many of the game's greats. Ben Hogan, one of the greatest players who ever lived, was famed for his powers of concentration on the course. He had an icy stare, made very little conversation with his playing partner or indeed his caddie and often just puffed away on a cigarette deep in concentration. It was noted that before hitting the ball he would stare into the distance, then turn and select his club, before hitting what was usually a perfect shot.

He never discussed the mental side of his game, and as a player he was something of an enigma – no one really knew his secret. He once told a journalist that the secret was found in the dirt. By this he meant time spent on the practice ground. Up until the time he died, he continued to practise in search of the perfect swing. One thing is sure: he practised harder than any of his fellow professionals. He practised until his hands ached, and then he practised some more.

However, a few years after his death a booklet was found in Hogan's study. It had been printed in the 1930s and was concerned with mental strength and mental conditioning. Many sections had been underlined in pencil, indicating that he had understood the need to develop a strong mind and strong muscle memory as the foundation for his greatness.

> **'When I come down the stretch, for some reason I have been able to keep myself together. My attention span gets more acute; my focus is better.'**
>
> Jack Nicklaus

DON'T MISTAKE MENTAL STRENGTH FOR FOCUS

Many people assume that, because they have mental strength, it automatically follows that they have good powers of **focus**. Although the two appear similar in many ways, they are not the same thing. Mental strength is the capacity to keep a higher level of concentration without being distracted. On the other hand, **focus**, in the *Silent Mind* approach to golf, is the ability to visualise the exact target we are aiming at (the final resting place of the ball).

So, when I speak about focus in the process of *Silent Mind* golf **I am not talking about our powers of concentration, but rather our powers of visualisation.** We need to look at a target in the distance and actually visualise our ball in the place where we want it to come to rest. However, once we have mastered **focus** in our pre-shot routine, any mental strength will only increase the chance of a successful outcome.

In many sports there are competitors who are known for being 'tough'. They are hard to beat even when their backs are up against the wall; you just know they have it within themselves to lift their game and produce the seemingly impossible. Many of these players have been accused of 'mind games' and of trying to 'psych out' their opponents. This may be by ignoring their opponent on the first tee after the initial handshake, being cold and aloof, or some other action. This is often interpreted as being unsportsmanlike. There are players who do such things to gain a tactical advantage over the mindset of the opposition. However, there are others who are just mentally very strong and totally focused on the match at hand. They want to win, and intend to stay as mentally prepared for the battle ahead as possible.

Jack Nicklaus and Tiger Woods are two players who exude confidence on the first tee. Nicklaus even used to say he felt one-up even before the match had begun. Both men are courteous to their opponents, but, make no mistake, their focus is absolutely on winning the match. To that end, they give all their concentration and attention to every shot they hit. Even their practice swings are part of a pre-shot routine.

The average person can focus, and clearly visualise the outcome of the shot they're about to hit. Yet many are easily distracted or prone to negative thoughts. When that happens, focus alone will be of no help.

You can see this on the professional tour. There are players who, when they get ready to hit a shot, seem to go into a trance; a low-flying helicopter, a car backfiring or a person shouting out from the crowd will have absolutely no impact on them. They probably will not even register the distraction and, in some cases, if asked about it later will not remember it happening. Yet there are other players who stand over the ball listening for the distraction. You see these players step away from the shot once, then twice, looking into the crowd and glaring at an over-enthusiastic fan, growing tense about something over which they have no control. When I think of these players, I honestly cannot think of one who has ever won a major.

THE ART OF FOCUS

Silent Mind is about being able to **see the target area in your mind's eye**. This becomes a point in the distance that your brain will compute as its objective. By allowing the brain to control the muscle memory required in a relaxed and unemotional state you give yourself the best opportunity to hit a perfect shot.

SEE IT ▶

Read the following paragraph. When you have finished reading it, I want you to close your eyes and visualise exactly what is described.

'I want you to imagine you are standing on the 18th fairway of your favourite golf course. As you look at the clubhouse you notice, directly above, 300 feet in the air, a red hot-air balloon. Beneath the balloon there is a basket in which there are three people who are waving at you.'

That's it.

I want you to now sit quietly with your eyes closed and try to visualise exactly what I've just described: a red, hot-air balloon floating about 300 feet above the clubhouse as seen from the 18th fairway of your favourite golf course.

Chances are that you are able to do that. You're able to have a vivid image of the red hot-air balloon and probably see three people waving at you. You have a clear image of the balloon above the clubhouse and, I imagine, you can see other aspects of the golf course that are familiar to you. The reason for this is because there is a part of our brain that allows us to visualise clearly an imagined scene.

However, **very few golfers ever visualise the shot they are about to play**. Instead, they talk to themselves and say something positive like, 'Hit a good shot.' Now that might seem like a normal thing to say; it's positive and instructive. The challenge is that our brain has a degree of difficulty in processing visually what a 'good shot' looks like, because 'good shot' on its own is an abstract concept. Therefore, you lack the mental instructions for the shot you are about to play.

On the other hand, if we also say (or think) something negative like, 'Don't hit it in the water,' or, 'Don't slice it into the woods,' or, 'Don't shank it,' we are giving our brain something specific to visualise. Our brain is now going to imagine exactly what we said: 'water; woods; shank,' but it will not visualise the word 'don't' because the word 'don't' is abstract and has no immediate visual description. So the *specific* negative instruction has taken the place of the *abstract* positive instruction in our mind's eye.

When we talk about **focus** we mean exactly that: **focusing on the outcome we want in a clearly defined visual picture we can see in our mind.** Some people have the ability to do this the first time; other people struggle, and there are a few who do not have the ability to visualise at all. When they close their eyes to try to see the red hot-air balloon they see only darkness. What they can do instead is get a clear sense of the red hot-air balloon. Though they cannot see it, they may be able to hear the noise we would associate with a hot-air balloon: the creaking of the wicker basket, the firing of the gas burner, or the sound of other players saying, 'Look at that red hot-air balloon.' Although not visual, this sense of the red hot-air balloon is still a point of focus for the brain. Some people learn visually (they see the outcome); others have a keen auditory sense (they cannot see the outcome but can hear it); still others learn kinaesthetically (they can sense the associated physical feeling or emotion).

If you were to ask a person who has been blind since birth to visualise a red hot-air balloon with three people in a basket, it would be impossible. Yet they might get a keen sense of what you are asking them to imagine. So when it comes to applying **focus** to your pre-shot routine, if, for any reason, it is impossible for you to clearly visualise the outcome, remember you are still able to get a sense of what you are trying to achieve, and that is enough for the brain to lock onto as its focus point.

'I close my eyes and see the shot. It's a
way of seeing the result before you do
it. I visualise the end result.'

Annika Sörenstam

FOCUS IN ACTION

Between shots, it is important to **walk at a pace that is relaxed and unhurried**, and to **breathe deeply** if you feel yourself tightening up. When you feel yourself getting nervous or tense, think back to a great shot you have hit earlier that round or in previous rounds, and remember the emotion it created, recall that state and feel it again. Do not get ahead of yourself by anticipating all the problems you may face in the next shot; your brain has all the computing power to make that calculation very quickly for you when you get to the ball.

When you arrive at the ball, stand behind it and look at the target area where you want the ball to end up. Look at this spot for a few seconds only, then select your club. If you find yourself between clubs and really cannot decide which club to use, I would advise you to **go with the club that instinctively feels right**. Your brain has already computed all the conditions and intuitively put into your conscious mind the best club for the shot. Of course, it will not always be the right club. Sometimes you make the perfect shot and it comes up short or goes long. The important thing is to remain confident and, when you find yourself with a shot where you're between clubs and really cannot decide, then apply good course management and take the club you believe will be the lower risk option.

Once you have selected the club, go through your pre-shot routine. If you do not have one I would recommend you go and see your local professional and discuss with them a good pre-shot routine for you.

My own routine is simple. Once I have selected the club, I approach the ball from the right-hand side, make a firm grip on the club and place the club-head behind the ball. I now look exactly at the focus point I have selected and 'see' the ball landing and coming to rest there. I take a full practice swing and give the club a short waggle to take away any unconscious tension in my arms and body. I am now ready to go. I look one more time at the focus point to make sure it is clear in my mind's eye. To use the analogy of an archer, I have got the arrow on the string and the bow is not yet pulled up into the firing position, but the target has now been locked in. This is my preparation for what comes next: perfect execution. It couldn't be easier.

I often find people are confused by the simplicity of what I have just described. Some people want it to be complex and semi-mystical; others just don't get it because they think this is what they are already doing. However, though they think they are going through this routine, or something like it, I doubt they really are.

Many people find it hard to focus in any capacity because their brains and thought processes are just too busy. **We need to be relaxed to focus and visualise clearly.** People walk too quickly to the ball and think too much about what they have to do without engaging their imagination at all. How often have you watched a golf competition on television where a professional hits a miraculous shot? We hear the commentators enthuse about the brilliance of the player's imagination, their ability to see something that others don't – a gap in the forest, a high flop shot over water, cutting a three-wood 260 yards out of light rough. These shots are not random flukes; they are first imagined and seen in the player's mind's eye, before the club is ever swung.

THE HURDLES TO FOCUS

Since I was four years of age I have played thousands of rounds of golf with hundreds of people. Though I am not a qualified golf teacher, and (other than a few trusted friends who have asked me to comment on their swing) would never give advice to anyone on technique, I have, I believe, uncovered the number one fault with most average club golfers, a few high-ranking amateurs, and even a number of professionals as well.

Too many golfers are in too much of a hurry to hit the ball.

By that I mean they concentrate their efforts on hitting the ball, and not swinging the club. We see high-ranking professionals, after a disastrous hole, stepping onto the next tee and attempting to murder the ball out of pure rage; there's no thought of a balanced swing and relaxed tempo.

It was about three years ago that I stopped trying to hit the ball. I figured the golf club was designed to hit the ball and nature designed me to swing that club. So long as I kept my part of the bargain I could trust the golf club to keep its part of the bargain.

It is important to understand the other hurdles that inhibit our ability to focus, time and time again, over a four-hour round of golf. Here are the three major offenders:

1. Negative Mindset

We approach the shot with a negative mindset. We don't mean to; we just do it out of habit or mood. This may take the form of telling ourselves exactly the shot we don't want to hit, or arriving at the shot with an absolute belief we will hit a bad shot. I don't need to remind you of the number of times after you have played a bad shot you have said, 'I just knew I was going to do that!'

In any stressful or competitive situation where we start thinking about what we need to do, there is an internal dialogue going on. This is the internal voice of the conscious mind making us aware of all the possibilities that lie ahead of us, and the consequences of each option. It brings to our attention the stronger emotional outcomes, which are negative scenarios. If we listen to this internal chatter it will influence our ability to stay focused and relaxed and play our best golf. Therefore, it is important to learn how to tune out all the chatter, and simply to stay calm and in a positive frame of mind.

2. Natural Impulse

Lurking within every player is a prehistoric person who sees a golf ball as food and the golf club as the jawbone of an ox (a primitive club). With that club they are going to beat the food by hitting it hard. In fact, they are going to hit it so hard it's never going to get up. Then they can take it home and cook it for supper and share it with their family in the cave. I believe that the natural impulse for many players is to try to hit the ball rather than concentrate on simply swinging the club.

3. Lack of Confidence

Many players do not believe they have the ability to hit the shot required. No matter how wide a fairway may look, it's not wide enough. No matter how short the putt, they cannot see the ball going in the hole, because in the back of their mind lurks the nagging doubt they're not up to the challenge. But the good news is that **confidence is a muscle we can build**, *if* we learn to focus on good shots and recall them and remember them in times of pressure.

We have to stand over a difficult shot and tell ourselves we can make that shot and **believe we can**. That way we will build our confidence. Even if we do not execute the shot as we wished, we can take away as something positive the fact that we felt confident, and recall it in the future. We must always seek the positive in every situation and use it to build and not destroy our confidence.

FAITH

YOU GOTTA HAVE FAITH

Faith is the ability to believe in something for which there is no real evidence. Every religion is based upon the notion of having faith in the existence of an unseen God. Our relationships with friends, family and other people are based on faith and trust. When we have faith we accept something to be true and make decisions based on that acceptance, without knowing for certain.

Faith lies at the heart of our confidence. The word confidence comes from the Latin *cum-fides*, which literally translated means 'with great trust'. A more common interpretation is 'with faith'. **In *Silent Mind* golf, faith in ourselves is critical to the successful realisation of our swing.**

How often in your life have you gone out and hit the ball exactly where you wanted it to go? How often have you gone out and played a match where you felt as though every club was a shovel and even putts of under 18 inches were hit more in hope than conviction? The brain is a beautifully complex and sophisticated organ. It tries to bring into realisation the thoughts you have imagined. **If you believe something to be true, the brain will look for evidence to validate that belief. In the absence of any evidence, it will help you make it true.** Isn't that great? It is why some people who are positive in their outlook towards life are always happy and see the good in every situation, while others who are negative in exactly the same situation find faults and things to complain about.

Let's look at a simple example. Suppose you're about to play a very important match that you really want to win. You're emotionally connected to this match; the person you're playing against is someone you don't like. In your mind, winning becomes more and more important. So without realising it you don't actually focus on winning, rather you focus on *not* losing. Without knowing it, you have set up an internal sabotage mechanism that will activate as required to validate your belief.

I have seen excellent players fall apart. They tell me the wheels came off, or they went into meltdown. Without exception, it has been my experience that when players start to play badly their opponents start to play well. As one person's **faith** in himself falls away, the other's is building shot by shot.

Let's go back to the match with the person you don't like, who you really want to beat. For the sake of this example let's say you are a good putter. You have a strong repeating stroke; however, on the first green you overcook your first putt and the ball races four feet past the hole. As you walk up to the next putt you say to yourself, 'I must not miss this putt.'

Your brain is already ahead of you as you're thinking about negative outcomes. Whether you make the putt or not, you have emotionally lost **faith** in your stroke. If you miss the putt, chances are you will say to yourself, 'I just knew I was going to miss that.' If you make the putt, you will probably think you've just been lucky and continue to look for the evidence that you're having a bad day on the greens. In the absence of evidence to the contrary you will subconsciously start to make bad putting strokes. **At all times, you must have faith in your ability to make the shot that you are attempting.**

> ## 'Good putters believe they are good putters.'
>
> Curtis Strange

YOU'RE IN THE WAY

Have you heard the expression 'getting out of your own way'? We intuitively know what 'getting in your own way' means; it is when we try too hard to let things occur naturally, when we try to control all aspects of our movements, and so in the process inhibit natural flow.

A simple example would be watching a young child walking across a kitchen with a bowl of soup. They are walking confidently and all seems well until someone, usually a parent (with the best of intentions), says, 'Don't spill it.' What happens? The child then starts to walk more slowly and concentrates entirely on not spilling the soup, the same soup they had been carrying with complete confidence only moments before. So, rather than let their actions flow (coordination, balance, muscle memory and focus), the child is now trying to control the actions that had previously allowed them to carry the soup bowl perfectly and with no thought whatsoever. They may or may not spill the soup, but the very act of trying hard not to spill the soup paradoxically increases the likelihood of them doing so.

We have discussed how complex the mechanics of the golf swing are, and yet **when we let the swing flow and trust it, more often than not we execute an acceptable shot**. So the challenge to us is, how do we 'get out of our own way'?

I had some insight into this when I was visiting a friend one summer evening. At his home in the back garden was a basketball hoop and on the lawn was the basketball. My friend David threw me the basketball and said, 'Have a go.' I had not thrown a basketball for 25 years and even then it was a very casual backyard game. It's not a sport I ever really played. I took the ball and, standing some 15 feet away, I pitched it towards the hoop with absolutely no expectation at all. The ball did not touch the sides and fell perfectly through the basket. My friend David was quite impressed and asked me to do it again. By this point I had walked five feet further away and was not intending to throw again, but as he had passed the ball I did. It was another perfect throw and went through the basket cleanly.

Intending to do something else, I had by now walked even further away when David threw the ball back immediately and asked me to try again. This time, a good 35 feet from the hoop, again without thinking, I threw the ball high and, for the third time in a row, it went cleanly through the hoop. David is an excellent (and competitive) athlete and has representative honours in a number of sports at a senior level. He started laughing and couldn't believe what he was seeing. To be honest, neither could I. I had never thrown such perfect hoops. When I got the ball for a fourth time, I moved closer and told him, 'Watch this.' Now I started to concentrate hard. I thought about every aspect of the throw: my balance, my body position, launch angle, wind direction – you name it, I was thinking about it. When I threw the ball it missed the basket by a good two feet.

I understood then, as I do now, that conscious thought during physical actions is probably going to be more of a hindrance than a help. In golfing terms, it is the same: the mind is always looking at the hazards and the problems related to the shot. **We frequently fail to trust our swing and therefore feel we need to control it by overriding our instinctive abilities.** The reason we do this is because it is difficult to keep our mind on the result, because our focus has gone from outcome (the target) to process (swing technique).

> ## 'The game is simple when you don't get in your own way.'
> Andy North

YOUR SWING IS YOUR SWING

There are as many different types of swing as there are people playing golf. Some upright, others very flat, some short and fast, others long and slow (that's me, by the way). Some are very mechanical in style while others flow with the artistry of a ringmaster demonstrating his prowess with a bullwhip. **As long as you have learned the basics of the golf swing, the interpretation you put on it is of importance only to you.** So, while your swing may not be textbook, or technically perfect, it is *your* swing and it is essential that you have faith in it. It is okay to admire aspects of other golfers' swings – a balanced tempo, the follow-through or slow take–away – and even to incorporate into your swing aspects of other people's that you believe will help you improve.

If there was a direct correlation between a perfect swing and golfing success, the top 100 golfers in the world would have the world's 100 most perfect swings. Clearly that's not the case. One only has to look at the diversity on the professional tour to see this. If you ever get the chance to watch vintage film of professional golfers in the bygone era of the 1920s and 30s, you will see that many of them have swings that would be ridiculed in the modern day. We must take comfort from the fact that there is such a diversity of swings: the evidence demonstrates clearly that there is not a 'one size fits all' construction.

The ball has no knowledge of how the club was swung; it responds only to the strike. However, to produce a consistent strike we need a consistent swing. The more we think about the swing while we are swinging, the less likely we are to create a consistent, repeatable swing. However, the more **faith** we have in our swing, and the more we are willing to trust it and not consciously interfere with it, the more consistent it will become.

> **'The biggest thing we fight in golf is tension. You have to let the body perform what it's supposed to do.'**
>
> Ken Green

WHICH WAY DOES IT BREAK?

We have all had a putt that was very difficult to read. We look at it from one side, then the other. Eventually we convince ourselves that it might break this way – or, if we read it wrongly, that way! In a situation like this, it actually doesn't matter too much if we read the putt rightly or wrongly. **If we are unsure about the putt, we will not hit the ball with any confidence, which will only plant further seeds of doubt in our mind.**

When we miss short putts we rapidly lose confidence in our putting stroke. How often in a round of golf is it those clutch three-footers which young children and old players seem to knock in as a matter of routine that make the difference to a score? In their early careers many of the best golfers in the game, including Arnold Palmer, Ben Hogan,

Sam Snead and Tom Watson, seemed to be blessed with the ability to 'will' the ball into the hole. Watson and Palmer in particular would boldly hit the back of the hole with every putt, even the short ones; when they missed they would go three or four feet past, certain in the knowledge that they would knock the return in. They appeared to be supremely confident, and the reason was – they were. Yet as they got older it was their putting that deserted them. Snead developed a form of putt that was subsequently banned, and Hogan used to freeze over the ball, unable to draw the club back. And just think of the putt that Tom Watson missed at Turnberry in the 2009 Open. It was a putt which earlier in his career he would have expected to make as routine.

It may have been years of competition that wearied the fine twitch muscles of these great golfers, but it happens to young professionals as well. They become more and more fearful of missing, and with that fear their faith in their ability to putt confidently diminishes.

I have discovered over the years that I make the majority of the short putts I expect to make and generally miss the short putts I expect to miss. This comes down to a matter of faith in my ability over the putt. With hindsight, if I think I'm going to miss a putt I usually do. I'm not being clairvoyant; I'm simply putting without confidence. We cannot read every putt correctly, but we can make a confident putt. If we are uncertain over a putt it will not be a confident stroke.

It will help if we take as much pleasure in our putting as we do in our drives, or a crisp iron shot into a par three. Do not be afraid of putting. Enjoy it as much as any other part of your game. **The green is the place where we need to be most relaxed and in control of our stroke.** But if our self-talk is negative, **if we tell ourselves that we have a tough putt, then it is inevitable that we tense up and our sense of touch is the first thing to go.** How many times have you felt that your putter is like a shovel in your hands as you tell yourself, 'This is a hard putt to read'?

So keep a strong sense of faith in your stroke and your ability to make the putt you face. This obviously does not mean you will make every putt by telling yourself you can, but it stops you experiencing self-doubt and reduces tension. Most importantly – **enjoy your putting.**

> **'Confidence is the single most important factor in this game.'**
>
> Jack Nicklaus

EVERY PUTT IS AN EASY PUTT

Every putt is exactly the same putt. You hit the ball with your putter and the ball goes straight. What determines the direction and distance of the putt is how well you read the green and how hard you hit the ball.

We all know people who are particularly good clutch putters: players who not only make more of the short 'must make' putts than others but, more importantly, *expect* to make them. Many years ago I played in the Atlantic Cup, an annual match between Europeans and Americans which takes an eight-a-side, Ryder Cup format. We were all average club golfers, but the games were taken very seriously, and tense affairs they were too. In the European team we had a player called Jeremy who was a very good putter. Jeremy would greet any putt of less than 16 feet by rubbing his hands together and announcing loudly, 'I fancy this.'

Jeremy would settle over the putt and send it on its way. If the ball didn't drop it was always stone dead and a 'gimme'.

For their part, the Americans had a player called Mike who was equally deadly on the greens. Mike's putting was so good that he considered anything within five feet as a 'gimme'! If Mike had a four-footer, he would look at his opponent and say, 'What's the matter, you got lockjaw? You know I'm going to make this.' And then he would roll it in. We would then tell him that the only reason we made him play was because we loved to watch his master class in putting.

For Jeremy and Mike every putt was easy. They had the right mindset. They approached every putt with a very positive mind, with faith in their judgement and stroke and believing that they *could* make the putt. Whenever they missed, there was no upset, sometimes a look of puzzlement, but never self-recrimination.

You must have faith that you can make a shot. And this faith applies to the putt more than any other shot on the course.

Approach every putt as a straightforward, easy putt. **Do not put doubt in your mind by describing it to yourself as tough or difficult or tricky.** When you make the shot, **expect that you will hole the putt** – or, at the very least, that you will leave the ball close.

If you can **put your faith in your putting stroke**, trust it and stay relaxed while you make the shot, you will notice a significant improvement in a very short time.

'The mind messes up more shots than the body.'

Tommy Bolt

PRESENCE

MINDFULNESS

Mindfulness is **being fully aware in the present moment**. Understand the link between your thoughts and emotions, and as you manage your thoughts you will be able to affect or control the associated emotion.

However, mindfulness is not something we achieve by sitting crossed-legged on a mountain top, deep in meditation. On the contrary, it is an *activity* – that can be done at any time, in any place, without any special technique. It is achieved simply by **bringing the mind to focus on what is happening in the present moment, the 'here and now'.** We can still be aware of the mind's usual background thoughts, but without associating any emotional value to them.

In the *Silent Mind* approach to golf, we need to be in a state of mindfulness in which there is no thought at all. I call this **presence**. We become totally absorbed in the moment, a state where we have no thoughts of the past or future, and, importantly, no thoughts in the present moment (which is simply the duration of the swing).

I've heard of professional golfers who are asked about the greatest round they ever played. Many tell of a stunning round of perfect golf during which they were 'in the zone'. When asked years later what they felt about that round, they remember it as being their best ever, but when asked how they felt at the time, they reply, 'Nothing.' Rather than odd, I find this wholly consistent with the state of perfect mindfulness – a state in which we no longer associate any emotion with the act of doing, or the outcome of the action. We exist in the moment, which explains why people in this state (psychologists explain it as 'optimal flow') feel 'timeless', with a strong sense of certainty of achieving the desired results.

It isn't easy to reach such an extreme degree of exactness, but the more we are aware of the conditions required to bring it about, the more likely we are to make it occur. As we stand over the shot, **the ability to think of nothing at all is the single greatest mental key to peak performance**.

It's like taking an exam. If you prepare over weeks through diligent revision and structured learning, you will have the knowledge required when you sit to take the test. All you have to do at that point is put it down on the paper.

The same is true of learning to be mindful. If you read this chapter and say to yourself, 'Oh, I get it,' that will help a little, but **structured learning and dedicated daily practice are the keys.**

THE CHATTERBOX MIND

When we sit in front of a computer screen we generally give one specific item our full attention. Behind the screen the microprocessors and hard drive are running a number of other programs, making tens of thousands of calculations every second. We cannot see what is happening behind the screen, even though there is a phenomenal amount of data-processing going on. Imagine all these calculations were appearing on the screen at a rate of ten per second: we would not be able to concentrate on any one image before it moved on. Yet this is what happens when we have mental chatter in our minds. We are consciously thinking about too many different things at the same time.

Let's go back to the image on the computer screen. The screen gets our full attention and focus. What is happening behind the screen is of no consequence to us because we are not aware of it, so we do not think about it. If we apply this analogy to the golf swing, the screen represents the mental image of where we want the ball to be (**focus**), and the process that enables us to make this shot a reality takes place behind the focal point (the subconscious mind). This might sound complex, but in fact it is simple. We focus on the target and then think of nothing else: the process takes care of itself. This is the ideal. In reality, the problem comes when we do think about something else. This *something else* represents what I call the chatterbox mind. **We have to learn to control the chatterbox mind.**

All meditation and hypnotic techniques are based on the process of stilling the mind – emptying it of conscious thought. Some people find it much easier than others. Some spend a great deal of time learning to still their mind. The good news is that everyone can do it. However, like anything in life that needs to be learned, it takes repetition, dedication and diligent practice. **We learn to still our minds through repeated practice.**

Learning how 'not to think' might sound like a paradox, and it is unlikely we will get it right the first time. When we first try to sit in silence and think of nothing, thoughts will pop into our heads. Usually these random ideas and images will just appear in our conscious minds. Through repeated practice we learn not only how to still the mind at will, but also, when these random thoughts do appear, how not to pay them any attention or focus on them at all.

THINKING OF NOTHING ▶

I would like you to put the book down and sit upright in a comfortable position for ten minutes with your eyes closed. I want you to think of nothing at all. Absolutely nothing. I imagine, right now, you think this will be the easiest thing in the world to do. Some of you may think it is an opportunity to have a quick snooze, but this is not about going to sleep, this is about emptying your mind of thought. Ten minutes, eyes closed, without sleeping or thinking of anything.

What happened? I imagine for the first 10 or 15 seconds you may have been able to think of nothing and then, slowly but surely, random thoughts popped into your head. They may have been golf-related, or about what you're going to have for dinner this evening, a friend you have not seen for many years, a car you would like to drive, your boss at work, a song you have not thought about for many years, or a joke someone told you. Maybe you just were aware of your seat or felt very self-conscious that you were trying to think of nothing. Time slowed down, and when you opened your eyes (after what you had imagined was ten minutes) you discovered that maybe only four minutes or less had in fact elapsed.

There is a good reason why it is so hard to think of nothing. When we are born, our brains kick into life and start to operate our nervous systems. Thinking becomes second nature to us, and *not* thinking is an alien concept. The brain doesn't switch off – even when we are asleep, it generates dreams.

Once we have consciously learned to do something, such as walking, the process and muscle memory that enables us to walk becomes automatic and we no longer think about it. Unless, of course, we have to walk along a narrow pass, high up a mountainside, where the penalty of falling off is serious injury or death. The reason we start thinking about walking in this sort of situation is that the brain has made a risk assessment, then drawn our attention to the risk in order to control the actions needed to keep us alive.

When you're walking down the street, you're not thinking about walking. When you start a journey, you actively know where you're going, and without thinking, you walk in the direction of that destination. **In the game of golf, we need to swing our club in the same way we walk along the road, with no thought at all, just an awareness of where we want the ball to finish.**

> ## 'Thinking too much about how you are doing when you are doing it is disastrous.'
>
> Harvey Penick

STILLING THE MIND

We do not still the mind simply by telling it to 'be quiet'. The very act of telling ourselves to think of nothing requires thought. Rather, we learn to still the mind through practising 'silent meditation' and creating a trigger word that we associate with this stillness. The guided meditation CD that comes with this book will explain this in more detail.

Using the *Silent Mind* techniques of **focus**, **faith** and **presence**, it is only in the final stage, **presence**, that we actually enter the *Silent Mind* state, where no thoughts exist, just being and doing.

As we walk up to the ball we assess all the factors that are going to influence the shot we need to make. At this point with *Silent Mind* we simply determine the focus point, the exact place we want the shot to finish. Once we have done this we select the club we need to take, and address the ball, with **faith** (confidence and understanding) that we are capable of hitting the shot we require. We place the club head behind the ball in preparation for the shot. It is at this point that we need to still the mind.

The most effective way to still the mind is by having a trigger word or action. The trigger word I use and recommend is '**presence**', but you should find your own word or action (a deep breath, maybe) that gets you into the state of not thinking. If you practise the meditation techniques on the accompanying CD (which I recommend doing for ten minutes every day), you will be programming your subconscious mind to respond to your trigger while in a deeply meditative and particularly suggestive state. Then, when you address the ball, you will be able to initiate the stilling of your mind with your mental trigger and so enter the *Silent Mind* state you have prepared for during your meditation sessions.

When I was a young boy I was told repeatedly to keep my eye on the ball at all times – I am sure you were too. If I hit a bad shot I would generally be told it was because I had my head up. When I used to play in tight matches, I remember I used to look intently at the back of the ball. What I was doing, without realising it, was concentrating my mind on one specific area, and in so doing, blocking out all thoughts.

However, when faced with a five-foot putt, which I simply had to make, no matter how hard I stared at the back of the ball, my mind would still be racing, with many negative thoughts about missing the putt flitting into my consciousness. Needless to say I usually did! As I have mentioned throughout this book, there is never any guarantee that we will hit the perfect shot, no matter how often we practise and how much we perfect techniques of mental conditioning. But, without any doubt, I can say **we will dramatically improve the probability of a good shot when we apply mental control and focus to our game.**

We learn to still the mind through practising again and again and again. Golf, like life, has no real long-term quick fixes. What we put in on the practice ground we generally get out on the golf course. The time and energy you spend learning to still your mind early in the morning or evening, if practised repeatedly, will give you a huge advantage on the course.

I was once told by a seasoned player that **halfway through a round of golf was not the place to practise.** I would add that **neither is it** a place to start trying to still your mind if you have not trained your mind to respond in the first place.

'The more vacant the mind is,
the better the play.'
Sir Walter Simpson

BREATHE

When I learned to skydive, the first lesson that was impressed upon me was to relax. To fall successfully and safely through the air at 120mph requires that you be relaxed and flexible, not tense and stiff.

Let's put the skydive in context. You are about to exit an aeroplane two miles above the earth with a parachute strapped to your back. You will fall for approximately 60 seconds and then, while remaining in a stable, belly-to-earth position, you will deploy your parachute. You hope your parachute will open, but are aware that if it doesn't you will be required to engage emergency procedures. The best way to get through this process as smoothly and safely as possible is to be aware and relaxed.

This is easier said than done. It is counter-intuitive to be relaxed about jumping from a plane, but it is exactly how you have to be to do it well. I have learnt from many people over the years that **the single most effective technique for performance-based relaxation is to control your breathing.**

Later in my skydiving career, I began to try more advanced techniques of flying my body. My instructor would continue to reinforce the importance of breathing and relaxing. As we climbed out of the aircraft and faced each other in the slipstream, my instructor would always point to his mouth to remind me to take a deep breath. When we are tense, nervous, or in a state of great concentration, we often simply stop breathing.

When two players are neck-and-neck coming down the final holes of a match, be it a local club competition or the last hole of a Major, the player who has learned to manage that pressure in a positive or constructive way is most likely to win. To manage the pressure, we first have to learn how to manage ourselves, and we do this by taking control of the adrenaline flowing through our bodies. It is not a mystery, it is basic human physiology. If we can control our breathing we will slow our heart rate; this will counteract the influence of the adrenaline which is causing this response in the first place. As our heart rate slows, the feelings of fear, panic and tension will dissipate.

MY FINAL ROUND FOR SURREY UNIVERSITY

As I mentioned in the introduction, I played college golf in England in the 1970s. College golf back then was very much an amateur game. Teams received no sponsorship of any kind and the handicap range of our team was between one and 20.

I believe I still hold a golfing record at the University of Surrey, which I suspect will be very hard to beat.

In two years I played 24 matches for the university golf team. When I was in a singles match, I always believed I would lose. This mind-set is now so alien to me that I cannot imagine I ever had it, but I did. Having suffered straight losses in my first three or four singles matches, I put a jinx on myself. I believed that under pressure my swing would not hold up. I simply convinced myself that the other person would win. Even if I was five up after nine holes, I consistently told myself that the blow-up would come. I never told myself I could win. Instead I always believed I would lose. I could physically feel myself tense up. My swing got shorter and shorter, then faster and faster. I would take short, shallow breaths and walk quickly to my ball. I was doing everything wrong.

I expected to lose; I had negative thoughts. I had no **faith** in my swing or my ability to win. I didn't need to tell my opponent that I lacked confidence because I manifested it in a hundred different ways. What I am about to tell you now is very important when seeking to improve your game of golf – not to mention any aspect of life.

Anything we can learn, and have learned, we can unlearn.

Coming into my final match, I had played 23 singles matches for the University of Surrey over a two-year period – and lost each and every one of them. The harsh fact, irrespective of how many of my short putts had horseshoed out of the hole or how many of my opponents had chipped in from 30 yards to snatch victory, was that I had crumbled. I was not the victim of outrageous misfortune – I had lost my self-belief.

My final match was against another university in a regional competition. In the morning we played a four-ball format, then went to lunch. My captain was very keen, as indeed were all my team-mates, that I should taste victory just once in my university career in a singles match. I was in complete agreement with them. My captain came up to me at lunchtime and told me he had requested I play against a member of the other team who he had discovered had a handicap of 18.

At the time my handicap was seven, and, because this was an official university match, it would be played without strokes being given. We would be playing level. He added, with a conspiratorial tone, that he had been plying this man with both red and white wine throughout the meal and had just bought him a beer in the bar (college golf in the UK back in the 70s . . . those were the days!). For my final singles match and last chance at a victory, he had set me up to play a slightly drunk 18-handicapper. Even I knew this was within my reach. We were to be the last match out; the captain had arranged this to put me under no pressure as regards the outcome of the event. At the appointed time, I met my surprisingly sober-looking opponent on the first tee. We duly exchanged pleasantries and, in the time-honoured tradition of the game, we courteously shook hands. He told me that he didn't usually play in these matches but that his side had experienced a late drop-out, so he was asked to step in at the last moment. I could barely contain my glee.

As he was a visitor he had the honour on the first tee. I remember he walked on to the tee with a three-wood. He dropped the ball on the turf and did not bother to tee it up, which I thought was a clear indication he was still intoxicated. He took a short practice swing, looked down the fairway, and swung. It went off like a rifle shot, with a low trajectory that climbed slowly but steadily until the ball landed some 230 yards down the middle of the fairway. This didn't faze me too much, because I appreciated he was relaxed from the wine, and it was more luck than design that he had hit such a good shot. I followed him with my tee shot and we both made par at the first hole. He continued to play what, I had no doubt, was the best golf of his life. We got to the turn all square and we were both one over par. I congratulated him on how well he was playing, but knew it would not last. It was only a matter of time before he started to choke and crumble.

The game continued at a very high level; there was never more than one hole in it. I won the 16th hole and was one up with two to play. I was preparing for my first, glorious, sweet-tasting victory after my two-year famine. I was relaxed and actually enjoying myself. I was in no doubt that victory was mine. As we walked to the 17th tee I casually asked my opponent where he normally played his golf. This is where it got interesting. He gave me the name of a course I knew to be a championship course, but not near his university. When I enquired further, he told me he was now a post-graduate student, and had been an undergraduate student at Cambridge University where, he added, he played in the university's first team. As I was computing this information and trying to make sense of it, I noticed one member of my team standing up by the green after his match. He had decided to come and support me and see how we were getting on.

I smiled as my opponent told my team mate that I was one up. As we walked to the tee box at the 17th hole I was trying to make sense of what my opponent had said about Cambridge University. I knew that the students in the Cambridge first team had handicaps between plus one and three. So, as casually as I could without my voice breaking, I asked him, 'What's your handicap?' As I was teeing my ball into the ground he replied: 'Two.' I almost choked as I spluttered out, 'Two!' He said, 'Well, not exactly, my exact handicap is 1.8.'

It occurred to me that my captain was the one who had got drunk at lunchtime, picked up the team sheet from the opposition, scanned all the handicaps, and seen a 1.8, which he thought was an 18. His attempt to hand this player to me like a lamb to the slaughter hadn't gone off as he had planned. I don't need to tell you what happened to my tee shot on the 17th. I lost 18 as well, and finished my university career with a record of played 24; lost 24.

As long as I believed I was the better player, I swung the club and played the game in accordance with that belief. As long as I believed I was going to win, I gave myself every opportunity to do so. But as soon as I discovered this man was a two-handicap golfer, that belief disappeared – and with it my swing and my confidence.

I now know that **the only person on the golf course you have to overcome is yourself**.

BELIEF BEFORE BEHAVIOUR

If you believe you are going to win, you greatly improve the probability that you will win. Likewise, if you believe you are going to lose, you increase the likelihood that you will lose.

Like most of the people reading this book, I've had my moments of glory and I've had my moments of quiet desperation. For example, in one competition I had a 25-yard chip shot over a bunker which simply became an impossible shot. For me in that instance, all I needed to do was get this ball over the bunker, but a small voice in the back of my mind told me, 'You're going to chilli-dip it into the bunker . . . or shank it . . . or stub it into the ground.' Every negative thought in the world poured into my subconscious mind rather than the one thought I needed: the belief that I could make the shot without any problem at all. Variations of this scenario have played out over the years.

Then I had a pivotal moment of enlightenment on the golf course.

Many years ago, I was playing in a match with some British friends against some Americans (like the Ryder Cup – except a lot more serious). My friend Tom and I were up against two Americans who were by far their side's toughest competitors. Both were single-figure handicappers as well as determined and competitive individuals. Though it was a social event, the matches were taken very seriously indeed. There was a lot of pride in winning, especially in the evening when speeches and match reports were given.

We tied the first three holes but then lost the fourth. On the walk to the fifth tee I began to think negatively (as was my mental habit, though I did not understand this fact at the time). I began to lose confidence and I believed the game was over. I began talking to Tom with a negative tone, lamenting the fact that we were going to lose. 'It's over,' I said. 'They're into their stride and their tails are up, I just know it.'

Tom had started poorly, which meant that my ball had been the scoring ball in the first four holes and even though I tied them on the first three, by losing the fourth, I'd begun the process of mental collapse and began to give up. Tom, on the other hand, later told me he had recognised that he was going to get worse before he got better, so had decided to become coach, supporter, motivational guru, Marine Corps Sergeant and playing partner all-in-one. 'You're joking,' he spluttered. 'We've got them just where we want them. You're playing as well as I've ever seen! Your tempo is metronomic and just a pleasure to watch. I've never seen you strike the ball so crisply, and that recent miss-hit had more to do with a bad lie than your swing.'

I played the next 12 holes two over par (at the time I was playing off a handicap of 12) and we won the match on the 16th (3&2). Tom had made me walk slowly between shots. He talked about everything but golf, and applauded every good shot I hit.

Even now, after 20 years, I remember three shots from that round. The first was a three-iron from 180 yards that I had to hook around some trees. To be honest, I didn't really know how to hook a ball to order in those days and I was never very confident hitting a three-iron. On that day, however, I gave absolutely no thought at all to the shot – other than the knowledge I had to hit a three-iron 180 yards and draw the ball over 30 yards. And I did exactly that. The second shot was a monster putt. I had to get it very close to have any chance of halving the hole. I was 20 yards off the putting surface going up two steps of slope on the green. I remember looking at the flag before I hit the shot with the full knowledge I was going to put it very close

– and I did. The third shot was to an island green with water on three sides. I didn't hesitate, and without a doubt in my mind, I swung my four-iron smoothly and confidently. It flew at the flag as though some on-board satellite navigation system was guiding it.

Each of these shots I just knew were going to be perfect, and though I was constantly under pressure, I was relaxed. I didn't think about it or try to figure out what had happened; little did I know that it would be over 12 years until I experienced that feeling again.

> **'When I got off the plane I told everybody I was gonna win this British Open. I didn't say it just once. I said it a hundred times, and saying something, you get to believe it. And once you believe it, it comes as no shock when you are out there leading the tournament. You take victory as your right.'**
>
> Lee Trevino at the 1971 Open Championship

THE PURSUIT
OF PERFECTION

GOLF'S HOLY GRAIL

What is it that makes the difference in those golfers who are immortalised as being amongst the 'greatest players' of the game? I have long been fascinated by those in life who achieve something that is way beyond the levels of success and expectation of the average person. In all fields of human endeavour there are extraordinary individuals who stand out from the pack, who raise the bar and who reshape our understanding of what is possible. Every age produces individuals like that, sportsmen who will take their place in the Hall of Fame and whose achievements will not be diminished by time. For example, in our current generation of sportsmen the heroics of Usain Bolt in athletics, Lance Armstrong in cycling, Roger Federer in tennis and of course Tiger Woods in golf will never be forgotten.

For many years my interest in golf was all about the technical side of the game. I thought if I could understand the technical side, the equipment, the swing mechanics, I would be able to master the mysteries of the game. I was obsessed with trying to hit the ball further with the latest club or tinkering with my swing using the latest tip I'd picked up in whatever golf magazine or instruction book I was reading.

Over the last few years, my understanding of the mysteries of the game has changed. I started to realise there was much more to be learned about how players became Major champions from the way they approached the game and their lives than there was from analysing their swing or obsessing about club technology. But what was it that made them successful over many other players who, on the face of it, had as good a technique and as much a chance of winning, but who wilted when the pressure was on as they came down the straight on a Sunday afternoon?

I started looking for clues as to *why winners win*. I wanted to understand what made these true champions perform at their best whilst under the severest pressure. What was their mental 'secret'?

I looked at a number of players who played their golf in an era before sports psychology and technological breakthroughs became the norm; players who did not have the benefits of video analysis. I wanted to find out what it was about their lives and their approach to the game that made them different, and made them great. I looked at three players in particular: Walter Hagen, Bobby Jones and Ben Hogan. I knew for each it would be different. But I also knew that the guiding principle at the heart of their 'greatness' would be the same. I was convinced I would find something common in all three of them which would be helpful to the average club golfer.

In this section, I show how everything at the heart of mental strength and performance management can be found in the behaviour and performance of past legends of the game. By understanding their success we can analyse what lies at the heart of consistent golfing excellence under the most severe pressures.

The professional game of golf in the UK and USA in the 1920s was played by blue-collar working-class men. Their status was that of skilled labourers, who were not allowed in the clubhouse of the members they served. They were known as the 'cracks'. Their job was to tend the greens, repair the clubs, teach gentlemen how to play and, when required, caddy for them. In those days tournaments were not only shorter but were played mid-week so the pro could return to his club for the weekend, which was the busiest time.

Even Open champions would return from a competition, trophy in hand, to life as a club pro, mending clubs and giving lessons. The professional game was not played by the members of the clubs, but by the skilled artisans, the club professionals. It came as no surprise to me to discover that the majority of the great tournament players were ex-caddies who had left formal schooling at an early age. Great players like Walter Hagen, Gene Sarazan, Ben Hogan, Byron Nelson and Sam Snead were all golfing greats who came to golf via the caddies' yard.

But equally there were a number of excellent amateurs around the same time, all of whom had come to the game as junior members of country clubs. Without doubt, the most famous of these was Bobby Jones, who won seven Opens and six National Amateur titles before retiring at the age of 28. He regularly beat the best professionals of the day.

Jones was very much a gentleman golfer. He hung his clubs up for the winter and did not really play recreational golf. For him the competition was everything. He played to test himself and to win. Jones was from an affluent professional background, and playing for money was at odds with his upbringing. His example demonstrates that it is not the nature of a player's motivation that counts, but rather the strength of that motivation allied to something else.

> **'To be consistently effective, you must put a certain distance between yourself and what happens to you on the golf course. This is not indifference, it's detachment.'**
>
> Sam Snead

BOBBY JONES

Bobby Jones was a sickly child who was unable to eat solid food until he was five years of age. When he was six years old he began spending his summers near East Lake Country Club. He was given a cut-down club, and his love affair with golf began. He showed an exceptional ability and quickly demonstrated his gift when he was nine years of age by winning the Atlanta Club Junior title. At 14 he won the Georgia Amateur title and also became the youngest player to qualify for the US Amateur. In his very first attempt at the US Amateur Title he beat a former winner, before being knocked out in the third round by the defending champion, Bob Gardner.

While Bobby Jones was learning to play, a Scottish professional called Stewart Maiden came to be the pro at the East Lake country club. Maiden was one of the famous 'sons of Carnoustie', who left the Scottish seaside town to travel the world and teach golf. Maiden was Jones' first golf teacher, and Jones would follow him around the course, taking in everything about the Maiden swing and adapting it for his own. This swing, with very few changes, was what Jones used for the rest of his life.

Jones' exceptional golfing talents were soon recognised, and there was huge pressure on him to realise his potential by winning competitions. But it was to be seven long years, from 1916 to 1923, before Jones finally delivered, with tournament success.

During the 'lean years', even Jones himself began to wonder if he would ever win. While travelling to the 1921 US Open he asked his close friend and subsequent biographer O.B. Keeler, an Atlanta journalist, if it would ever happen. Keeler prophetically said, 'Bobby, if you ever get it through your head that whenever you step on the first tee of any competition, that you are the best player in it, then you'll win this championship and a lot of others.'

The breakthrough, when it came, was dramatic. In 1923 he won the US Open in a play-off against Scottish golfer Bobby Cruickshank. Jones then dominated the game of golf until his retirement seven years later at the age of 28. During his career, Jones won 13 of the 21 Majors he entered and, in 1930, became the only player to achieve the ultimate in golf by winning all four Major tournaments in the same year.

What is all the more incredible is that Jones was an amateur in every sense. He played no more frequently than the average club golfer. He reckoned he played a maximum of 80 rounds a year, and his golf was all played in a four-month season because he hung his clubs up in the winter and only played in other tournaments as a warm up for the majors.

In addition to his golfing accomplishments, Jones had degrees in engineering, law and literature. He created the Augusta National golf club with his friend Clifford Roberts and made it the home of the Masters tournament. Jones was the most famous athlete of his time and had the ultimate honour of having a hole named after him at St Andrews, the home of golf.

Jones was an individual who was able to rise above the norm and set standards for himself. When he felt he could no longer keep these standards he announced that he would retire. His legacy to golf endures to this day.

In 1929, the year before he won the 'Grand Slam', Jones turned his mind to the possibility of such a feat, and the faith and self-belief that he would be the one to do it. The Grand Slam was no fluke of circumstance, it was a mighty goal that Jones conceived, planned and executed, with total faith in himself.

> **'It is nothing new or original to say that golf is played one stroke at a time. But it took me many years to realise it.'**
>
> Bobby Jones

WALTER HAGEN

Walter Hagen's introduction to golf could not have been more in contrast with that of Bobby Jones. Hagen was born into a working-class family and started working as a caddy. He learned his golf by watching and imitating the swings of the better players he caddied for.

And, whereas Jones was a modest, retiring man, Hagen was a showman, a flamboyant character who knew from an early age he wanted to live his life on the big stage with as much style as possible.

Hagen was the first professional golfer to challenge attitudes to professional golfers, then thought of as skilled labourers who were somehow inferior to the club members they served. Hagen believed he was the equal of any man. And he won his first US Open, in 1914, when he was just 22 years old.

He was only able to enter the tournament because a member of the Rochester club, where he was the pro, generously offered to cover his costs. He travelled to the Midlothian golf club in Illinois by bus. The night before the tournament started he suffered a terrible bout of food poisoning, which left him weak and not really fit for play. But, as he did not want to let his sponsor down, he forced himself to the first tee and proceeded to shoot a first round of 68, breaking the course record. He then won the tournament by leading in all four rounds.

Hagen had grown up living a hand-to-mouth existence. A naturally gifted athlete, he was nevertheless prone to worrying about irrelevant things like the weather or how other players were doing, matters over which he had no control. It was said that, when he won the US Open in 1914, he was so weakened by the food poisoning that the only thought he could keep in his mind was his next shot. There was no room for any of his other anxieties. This taught him a valuable lesson, and thinking too much on the course was never an issue for Hagen again.

Essentially, Hagen had supreme confidence in himself. During that period in golf's development, professional golfers were attached to a club, which gave them a living throughout the year providing lessons and mending clubs. Hagen, however, became the first unattached golf professional when he announced that it was his intention to make a living solely by playing competition golf. He was also the first golfer to be aware of the power of advertising and the value of exhibition matches. But he also recognised that in order to maximise his value he had to be the best golfer in the game and he had to be a winner.

Hagen won the British Open championship at Royal St George's in 1922.

Yet, as a professional, Hagen was not allowed in the club house with the members. Hagen hired a Daimler limousine with a chauffeur. He parked the car in front of the club house and proceeded to use it as his changing room and dining room!

Hagen was the model of calm on the golf course. He had the wonderful knack of ignoring a bad shot and concentrating on his next one. He said he expected that in any round of golf he would hit seven bad shots. Without realising it Hagen was applying the very modern technique of 'positive psychology' and 'mindfulness' to his game.

Hagen went on to win 11 Majors and was generally considered the greatest match-player of all time. His philosophy towards life can still be summed up in his most famous quote: 'You're only here for a short visit. Don't hurry. Don't worry. And be sure to smell the flowers along the way.'

> **'You don't have the game you played last year or last week. You only have today's game. It may be far from your best, but that's all you've got. Harden your heart and make the best of it.'**
>
> Walter Hagen

BEN HOGAN

Ben Hogan is as much an enigma today as he was when he was playing. His upbringing was tough: like Hagen, he was born into a working class family. His father committed suicide when Ben was nine. Ben and his brother, Royal, had to go out to work to help the family make ends meet. Hogan's personality was very different from that of Bobby Jones or Walter Hagen.

When he was eleven years old, Hogan started caddying at the Glen Garden country club. It was a tough life. The new caddies had to compete with older, more established caddies for work. Like so many caddies before him, Hogan was fascinated by the game, and he started to teach himself to play by watching other players and using elements of their swings. Soon after his seventeenth birthday he turned professional and at the age of twenty he joined the then small touring professional circuit.

It was a challenging life and Hogan was frequently broke; he often came home from the tour with no money. His game was marred by a severe hook, which he claimed was so bad that he could get no lift in his four-wood and meant that any dog-leg-right hole was impossible for him to play. He solved these problems and went on to become considered one of the best strikers of the ball of all time.

Hogan worked so hard on his game that the adjective 'Hoganesque' became a byword for perfection. He was sometimes accused of being aloof or indifferent to his playing partners, but this was down to the intensity of his focus when he was on the course. Hogan was committed to practice and although he never had a swing coach he was known to seek advice from other players if he thought he needed it.

Commentators used to think that Hogan had the 'secret' to golf and they would ask him what that secret was. Hogan's answer was, 'The secret lies in the dirt', a reference to the amount of time he spent on the practice ground. He was known to practise for up to eight hours a day, and said that practice 'never bothered me the way it bothers some people'.

Like many great golfers, it took Hogan time to get on the winning trail, but when he did he became relentless. In 1948 he won 10 tournaments and during his career he won a total of 65 professional events, including nine Majors.

In 1949 Hogan was very seriously injured in a car crash and there were doubts about whether he would walk again, never mind play golf. But after 59 days in hospital he returned to the game.

Hogan possessed a fierce determination to win. His swing stood up to the severest tests and is still considered by many experts as one of the classic golf swings. Although he could be intimidating to play with, he was cordial and well mannered at all times, if a bit reserved and private. When Hogan retired he stepped away from the game and lived a very private life but still continued to practise every day!

> ### 'Placing the ball in the right position for the next shot is eighty percent of winning golf.'
>
> Ben Hogan

THE MASTERS CONCENTRATE

What these three great golfers, Hogan, Jones and Hagen, had in common was that they each went through a period of failure before their big breakthrough came. But, once they had their first wins, they seemed to be able to develop a mindset that worked on every shot, and thereafter achieved continued success. They identified what it was that allowed them to focus on their game. There is no doubt that they had complete faith in their own ability to hit the ball.

During his seven long lean years, Bobby Jones was one of the first golfers to be known as 'the best player not to have won a Major', and this reference to him in newspapers and magazines annoyed him. He was determined to get rid of that tag.

Jones knew that winning had everything to do with his state of mind. He had seen players in the toughest conditions wilt under the pressure and psychologically collapse.

Jones had, by his own admission, a terrible temper on the golf course. He was a bag kicker and a club thrower. He had been spoken to about this many times, but it wasn't until he realised that he had to control his emotions and his temper on the course that he came into his own. In the 1920 US Amateur, Jones was drawn to play against Francis Ouimet, a former caddy from Boston. Ouimet had stunned the golfing world in 1913 when, at the age of 20, he beat the then two best players in the world, Harry Vardon and Ted Ray, in a play-off to win the US Open.

Ouimet and Jones had met the previous year, and a firm friendship had developed. Francis was deeply admired by Jones and served as a role model for him. In particular Jones was impressed by Ouimet's very balanced nature and his calmness on and off the course, to such an extent that he determined to adopt the same approach in his own golf. Jones was still under pressure to deliver what everyone expected of him, but he was now a much calmer and more focused individual.

The 'shot heard around the world', which signalled his breakthrough and the start of his winning streak, happened on the final hole of the 1923 US Open at Inwood country club, New Jersey. Jones was in a play-off against Scottish professional Bobby Cruickshank. After an epic battle, the players were tied after 17 holes of the play-off.

The 18th hole at Inwood is a dramatic finishing hole. It is a long par-four guarded by a lagoon. To have any chance of reaching the green in two, players have to hit a long drive. For once, Cruickshank's drive was poor. He hit a low hook that travelled about 150 yards and meant that he could not possibly reach the green in two. Jones played his customary fade, a long shot that landed just off the right side of the fairway, but his ball was on a patch of dry hard ground surrounded by dirt. He had two hundred yards to the green over the lagoon.

Cruickshank had no option but to lay up, and he played his second shot to leave himself an easy pitch to the flag.

All of the accounts of the day say that Jones didn't waste any time over his second shot. He pulled his driving iron out of the bag – the equivalent of a two-iron, a club which is notoriously difficult to get right. Jones' father, his friend, the journalist O.B. Keeler, and his golf teacher, Stewart Maiden, could hardly bear to watch.

All three men said afterwards that they had never seen Jones play a ball with such decisiveness. The ball cleared the water, bounced twice on the green, nearly hit the pin and came to rest six feet past the flag. Jones himself said that he had no memory of the shot. He remembered looking up and seeing the ball on the green and wondering how it had got there.

For me, this is the single most revealing event in Bobby Jones' golfing career. He faced a difficult shot under intense pressure and executed it to perfection, yet he has no memory of the decision-making process he went through beforehand. He was what we would now describe as being 'in the zone' and experiencing what psychologists would describe as 'optimal flow'.

This, for him, would have felt like time standing still, as he instinctively made the right decisions, dismissed any element of worry from his mind and concentrated totally on the task in hand, as action and awareness combined and his subconscious mind took over.

The fact that Jones has no recollection of the shot is what convinces me that he was 'in the moment' and was playing golf in the purest possible way: without conscious awareness, emotional attachment or thought of any kind. His mind was silent. Under the greatest imaginable pressure, having never won a major, he faced a shot that in any situation would be very challenging and require perfect execution – and this is exactly what he achieved. I have no doubt that focus and presence were involved in this one shot. But more impressive still was Jones' complete absorption in what he was doing as, for a few moments at least, time stood still.

I can only speculate as to what really happens in the mind of a player at such a moment, but, given Jones' seven years of not winning, it seems as though a player can almost surrender to fate, to accept the outcome and remove a large amount of pressure in the process.

Hogan had a similar intensity of focus on his own game on the golf course. During a practice round for the Masters, he made a birdie on the par-three 16th. His playing partner went one better and made a hole-in-one. When they arrived on the 17th tee, Hogan turned to his playing partner and said, 'You know that is the first time I have birdied that hole.' He made no reference to his playing partner's ace.

This is not the behaviour of a grumpy competitive individual, but an example of someone so absorbed in his own game that he really doesn't see what is happening around him or with other players.

Jones also showed this capacity to ignore what was happening around him. In the final round of the 1926 British Open he was paired with Al Watrous, and they were tied for the lead. On the 17th hole, Jones hooked his drive into a bunker, leaving him 175 yards to the flag. Watrous found the middle of the fairway and proceeded to put his second shot on the green. Once again it looked as though Jones would fail to deliver on all that promise he had. With his ball in the bunker and his opponent on the green, his chance of winning the Open seemed to have gone. Under the most exacting pressure, Jones played a wonder-shot which landed on the green well inside Watrous' ball. Watrous then three-putted and Jones won his first Open.

It was said that Jones, the epitome of the gentleman golfer, the player who had more sense of fair play and etiquette than any other golfer of his time, did not once look at Watrous during the playing of this hole, or the entire round. For a man noted for his perfect manners, this seems odd – until we see it in the context of his complete focus and 'being in the zone'. Jones was simply totally absorbed in what he knew he had to do.

The best players have this focus and this intensity and this belief in themselves. Hogan very rarely asked his caddy for advice, and when he did it was usually for a second read on a putt. He was confident in his own opinions and his swing.

Hogan's breakthrough came in the 1946 US PGA Championship, which was then played as a match-play event. He was the underdog in the final against a player called Porky Oliver, who had already defeated the defending champion in the quarter-finals. Oliver was in great form and was by far the fans' and the bookies' favourite to win the tournament. After the morning round, Hogan was three down. He knew that if he was to have any chance of winning he had to be at his best in the afternoon. When the afternoon round started, it was noticed that Hogan was even more severe-looking than normal. He was grim-faced, and his mouth was tight.

It was generally felt that Hogan would not stand up to the pressure. He was already three down, and it seemed only a matter of time before Hogan, against a player at the top of his game, and under the stress of playing in the final of a Major, would crumple. But Hogan was made of stronger stuff. No one claims that great pros don't feel pressure, but what sets them apart is the way that they deal with that pressure. Hogan rose to the challenge. He played the front nine holes in 30 shots and then, with a succession of birdies on the back nine, pulled the game back and went on to win the match 6&4.

Hogan's style never changed. He would stare at the shot he had to make. He would take a final puff on the inevitable cigarette, throw it to the ground, pull the selected club decisively from the bag and immediately play the shot. He played quickly even when the shot was critically important, like the one-iron he played to the green in the 1950 US Open, in a successful attempt to force a play-off, which he eventually won.

Remember that Hogan played in an era before yardage books and golf satellite navigation systems. He had to trust his own estimate of the distance left to the flag, and he had to have confidence in his swing and his club selection. When Hogan stopped winning on the tour, it was not his driving or iron play that failed him. Until well into his fifties, Hogan was as close to perfection as anyone from tee to green. As so often with the best players it was his putter which let him down. He began to fear his putter. He would freeze over the ball, unable to draw his putter back. On occasions he was so lacking in confidence on the putting green that he would three-putt from distances of three or four feet.

Walter Hagen was a different kind of character from Jones and Hogan. Hagen loved the limelight. He was an extrovert with the wonderful touch of the showman about him, and always seemed to be enjoying himself on the golf course. Not for him the grim face or the pained demeanour. He relished the challenge, the atmosphere and the pressure of big tournaments. In fact, his preparation for some tournaments, including the US and British Opens, often saw him out on the town living it up the night before.

Jones, on the other hand, struggled with his nerves during competition and he was known to lose up to 20 lbs during a tournament because he was unable to make himself eat. Once, when Hagen, Jones and Francis Ouimet were playing together, Hagen said to Jones, 'What's the point of losing your temper, kid? It's only a game!' Jones was an engineer and had a highly analytical mind; his pursuit of perfection often came at great cost to his enjoyment of the game. Similarly, Hogan was a heavy smoker on the golf course and, like Jones, would eat very little during a tournament.

His temperament on the course may have been different from that of Jones and Hogan, but Hagen's will to win was every bit as great. But he reached the 'zone' in a different way from them. For Hagen, golf was a game. It came naturally to him. Like Jones, he was not an obsessive practiser. That didn't mean he didn't want to win. He was fiercely competitive, and for him winning on the golf course was everything. In 1926, when he finished a very respectable sixth in the British Open he dismissed it as 'another disappointment'. For Hagen believed that only winners were remembered; everyone else was an also-ran.

When on the course, Hagen had a very pragmatic approach to the game: he expected to hit every shot perfectly. But he was also a realist and knew from experience that in any game of golf at the very highest level you could expect to hit around seven poor shots. His mind was adjusted to this fact, so that when these shots came along he did not get angry with himself, and did not dwell on them. He filed the shot away, moved on and did not think of it again. That approach helped to clear his mind for the next shot and removed negative baggage.

A masterful short-game player, Hagen had a wonderful ability to get up and down from seemingly impossible positions. He was a natural and intuitive player, but I believe that the secret to his success was his relaxed manner, which enabled him to concentrate where it mattered, but also allowed him to withstand the stress which caused other players such problems when the pressure was turned up.

When you next watch a golf tournament, note how the top players concentrate over a shot. I am sure you also concentrate over your shots, but do you close out all external influences while you do so? To the extent that you shut down your mind, make it silent until the only thing which is there is the shot which you are about to make? Great players do this. They are able to become so focused that they do not notice the external factors which plague the average club golfer's game – background noises, trains whistling, crowds shouting, or even a dog running across the green in the middle of a putt!

Great players can focus intensely on the moment to the exclusion of everything else. The next time you play, try to do this for every shot.

> **'You create your own luck by the way you play. There is no such luck as bad luck. Fate has nothing to do with success or failure, because that is a negative philosophy that indicts one's confidence, and I'll have no part of it.'**
>
> Greg Norman

MASTERING THE PRESSURE

Ray Floyd once wisely remarked, 'Anyone who says they play better under pressure has never been under pressure.' Great players feel pressure as much as anyone else; anyone who wants to win knows what pressure is. What makes the difference is how they cope with that pressure in the toughest conditions, coming down the home straight in a Major tournament.

There have been many examples over the years of great golfers who never managed to deliver their early promise. In the 1920s, there was an immensely gifted golfer called Leo Diegel. Diegel was considered one of the great shot-makers of the game and was expected to win many Majors. He was famed for the devastating accuracy of his iron play. Golf writer Bernard Darwin called him the greatest golfing genius he had ever seen. In 1928 he won the Canadian Open and the US PGA.

Diegel was described as a sensitive soul with a hyperactive mind which got in the way of his golf and made him subject to nerves and over-analysis of what he was doing. He played himself into contention in many Majors, only to have his nerve desert him in the closing stages. In the 1925 US Open he was leading by three shots with six holes to play. He lost nine strokes over those six holes to finish fifth.

On occasions when I have played a coaching round with a professional, one of the comments the pro has often made to me is, 'Too many thoughts.' It seems Leo Diegel suffered from 'too many thoughts'. When Sam Snead was asked what he thought about when he was playing his best golf he famously replied, 'Nothing at all.' When a player is playing well in a competition he plays much more instinctively than analytically. Diegel, on the other hand, could not stop thinking about his swing. He was known to get up from a table between courses at a meal to make practice swings.

Diegel was so concerned by his inability to cope with the pressures of the final round of tournaments, where he would regularly play himself out of contention, that he took drastic action. He dramatically changed his putting stroke to a very unorthodox stiff-wristed, bent-over, elbows-out style. It seemed to help his putting, but no golfer then or since ever adopted his style. Diegel was the first player to seek the help of a psychiatrist to manage his overactive mind. This had an immediate effect, as he went on to win back-to-back US PGA titles in 1928 and 1929. But then he slipped back to his old ways.

So how did the great players of the game like Hogan, Jones and Hagen master their minds under pressure?

Jones had complete faith in his swing. He used his analytical engineer's mind to calculate the distance to the flag accurately and to read the slope and pace of the green. During tournaments commentators would often remark on Jones' appearance: he would look pale and ill, and it was known that he suffered from nausea, loss of appetite, anxiety and stress during a tournament. But at the crucial moments he was able to ignore all of these factors and concentrate on the task in hand.

The origins of this ability to concentrate may be traced back to a round Bobby Jones played in his first US Open. The tournament organisers paired the temper-prone 18-year-old debutant with the 50-year-old British golfing legend Harry Vardon, playing his last Open. Jones had seen Vardon play an exhibition match at East Lake seven years earlier and was thrilled to be playing with his hero. After their practice rounds Jones spent some time with Vardon talking golf.

When Jones teed up the next day he tasted the tension which golf at the highest level brings. He felt physically unwell and manifested all the signs of a panic attack. He shot a 78. In the second round he shot a 74 and was seven shots behind the leader. At that point Jones felt that he could not win the tournament and he relaxed. In his new, relaxed frame of mind, with the pressure off, he went out and shot 70, putting him back in contention. The nerves returned and in the final round he shot another 78. This gave him an eighth place finish, which wasn't bad for an 18-year-old in his first tournament. But more important was what he had learned: that he needed to develop a strategy to cope with the stress and enable him to play the way he had in the third round. He needed to know how to quieten his mind.

Walter Travis was an Australian amateur golfer whom many people considered the best putter of a ball who ever lived. He was a natural, who took up golf at the age of 35 and two years later reached the semi-finals of the US Amateur. He was also a natural pessimist. Because he expected things to go wrong, he did not get unduly upset when they did, and saw it as part of the game of golf. Travis always understood the importance of the mind in golf. In 1908 he founded the magazine *American Golfer* and in it he wrote:

'Always be on the aggressive, act as if you are quite sure of yourself, and never give an opponent the psychological advantage of imagining that you are the least afraid of him. Many a man is beaten before he starts by admitting to himself the other's fancied superiority and unconsciously conveying it in his general bearing. It only gives the opponent the slight encouragement which enables him to pull out a winner in a tight match.'

In 1924 Jones was able to secure a putting lesson from Travis. During this lesson Travis made important changes to Jones' putting style, but much more importantly he also advised Jones on how to cope with pressure. He told Jones to practise breathing-control, which would help negate the nervousness that afflicted him. Bobby Jones made the suggested changes and decided to do his best to go easier on himself and not be unduly upset by bad shots.

Hagen and Hogan coped in different ways. As we have seen, after his death it was discovered that Hogan kept booklets on mental strength and positive thinking in his study. It is clear that Hogan understood the need to control the mind, and I am sure that he applied many of the lessons he learned in those booklets.

Hagen was a fierce competitor who used his casual joking style to keep himself calm. He loved being centre stage so that when a critical shot had to be played he stepped up and savoured the opportunity. I think this goes some way towards explaining how he was able to hit miraculous recovery shots. On numerous occasions opponents thought they had won a hole, only to see Hagen hit an amazing pitch or hole a huge putt.

It's wrong to assume that the great players of the game did not suffer nerves or doubts about what they intended to do. It is just that they developed very strong compensating measures to remove or at least minimise those doubts.

> **'You swing your best when you have the fewest things to think about.'**
>
> Bobby Jones

THE HOGAN SECRET

It has always been a popular myth that Ben Hogan discovered the 'secret' of golf – that his thousands of hours on the practice ground had allowed him to gain a crucial insight into what made a golf swing work.

Hogan's swing was grooved so finely that he could repeat it consistently on the course and deliver exactly what he required every time. It was said of him that he never hit a shot in a tournament that he had not practised a thousand times before on the driving range. Tiger Woods has said that he believed only two golfers in history 'owned' their swings in this way. One was Ben Hogan and the other was a little known Canadian professional called Moe Norman. Norman was a reclusive player who suffered from what we would now describe as a form of autism. His health problems meant that he spent most of his career in Canada and played very rarely on the PGA tour.

But is there a secret?

If only golf were that simple!

All sorts of rumours existed about Hogan's 'secret' during his triumphant years. He was treated as if he had discovered the secret of alchemy and could turn base metal into gold. In the 1950s *LIFE* magazine was reputed to have entered into a contract with Hogan whereby he would share the secret with their readers. This was encouraged by suggestions he would retire, after losing the 1955 US Open in a play-off to an unknown golfer called Jack Fleck. But Hogan was not the kind of man who would retire as long as he believed there was any chance of winning.

Hogan recognised the importance of publicity. Long before rock stars like the Beatles or Bob Dylan or sports stars like Eric Cantona perfected the art of giving enigmatic answers to questions, Hogan became an expert at deflecting questions. When up-and-coming golfer Ben Crenshaw asked him how to hit a low-running shot Hogan replied, 'Hit it on the second groove.' In response to a journalist who asked how to improve his game he replied, 'The only thing a golfer needs is more daylight.' This inclination towards enigmatic statements suggests talk of a 'secret' may have been an early piece of sports mythology.

Yet it was apparent that Hogan was one of the best strikers of a ball the world had ever seen, so his contemporaries and fellow professionals all had their own theories about his secret.

For Mike Turner it was Hogan's *grip*. Fred Gronaur declared the secret was all in his *pivot*. Claude Harmon believed it was his *hip turn*, while George Fazio thought it was to do with his shoulder maintaining *a level attitude* throughout the swing. Interestingly, these theories are all about the technical aspects of the game. The great Sam Snead didn't think there was any secret at all. But perhaps it was Gene Sarazen who got closest to the secret when he smiled, pointed to his head and said, 'Ben thinks better than anyone who has ever played this game.'

Hogan had already published a best seller called *Power Golf* on his attitude to the game. Henry Luce, the well known US publisher, decided it was time to update the book and he encouraged the magazines *LIFE* and *Sports Illustrated* to bid for the serialisation rights. *Sports Illustrated* won the rights and published excerpts from the book where Hogan announced that in his opinion the secret to his swing was 'pronating' the left wrist on the backswing.

Hogan wrote that this was based on a 'Eureka!' moment he had had while remembering what the old Scottish professionals taught. It involved allowing the hands to rotate to the right until the left hand was almost pointing straight up at the top of the backswing. Hogan then weakened his left hand on the grip by moving it a quarter of an inch to the left, which allowed for greater rotation of the hands on the backswing. Although hugely technical, this explanation of pronation thereafter became the accepted revelation of Hogan's secret.

It was a difficult concept for the average club golfer to understand. Frankly, I doubt its truth: I believe there was no secret. When Hogan agreed the huge advance of $30,000 for the serialisation rights to the book I think he knew he had to deliver something to a public who had been clamouring for his secret for years – and he fixed on 'pronation'. In fact I suspect Hogan's secret was just that he was 'the complete golfer' – a player who had such an acute feel for the game and such mastery of his swing that he played the game as perfectly and intuitively as it had ever been played up until that point.

Hogan *was* technically brilliant at golf and he had an ability to produce any shot on demand. If there was a secret to his golf it was this ability to produce the right shot at the right time – and the confidence it gave him in his approach. His technique and belief in himself were so strong that he had no negative thoughts when he made the swing. For this reason Hogan may still be the perfect golfer.

Hogan's nickname was the Hawk. When he was on the course the intensity of his stare was like a hawk fixing its gaze on a distant prey. Like a hawk, Hogan was oblivious to anything else which was happening around him. He was visualising in his mind the shot he intended to make, where he wanted the ball to go and the distance he had to hit it. And, like a hawk, once he had made this mental calculation he carried it out with precision. Not a technical trick, then, but a consistent mastery of the mental game, built upon the foundation of a solid technique which he could repeat at will under pressure.

One of the major benefits of the digital age is that we are now able to look at the swings of the golfing greats whenever we want. I recommend studying the swings of Hogan and Bobby Jones. You will be able to compare the differences between Hogan's tight compact precise swing, and Bobby Jones' narrow stance and loose willowy flow. Their techniques could not be more different, but their minds – their attitude and ability to focus, to be in the moment – were exactly the same.

> **'Golf is twenty per cent talent and eighty per cent management.'**
>
> Ben Hogan

INSIDE THE CHAMPION'S MIND

A champion golfer has to learn to cope with the pressure that comes with winning, but it is said that you need to learn how to lose before you can win.

For both Ben Hogan and Bobby Jones that was true. They both took a long time to realise their potential and they both learned to cope with serious problems which could have destroyed their golfing careers. Hogan had to deal with a very damaging hook: he developed a grooved swing during hours of practice which eliminated the hook. Jones had to learn to overcome the strain which his perfectionist mindset brought to him.

The challenges Hogan and Jones faced show the two key aspects of becoming the best golfer you can be: the swing and the mind. First you need to have a golf swing you can trust as a solid foundation. Second, you have to cultivate the mind of a champion.

Different sports stars have used different approaches to create the mindset of a champion. While there is no surefire route to get 'into the zone', no distinct technique that separates a great champion from the rest, it is possible to identify three key mental qualities which are common to great champions, and which 'normal' sports players such as you and I can develop in order to transform our mindset into one of a champion.

To be a champion requires **ambition**. Succeeding at the highest level of sport involves dedication, sacrifice and, most of all, a burning desire to win. When Seve Ballesteros entered his first professional tournament, the Spanish Professional Championship, at just sixteen and a half years of age, he didn't own a driver and used a three-wood off the tee. In the first practice round he played the front nine holes in 27 shots and in the tournament proper finished in a very respectable 20th place. But 20th wasn't good enough for him: back in the locker room the frustration boiled over and Seve began to cry. A seasoned professional tried to console him and told him that he had done very well. Seve's reply was, 'Yes, but I came to win.' Ballesteros entered every tournament to win it: that was his focus, his expectation and his desire.

Allied to *ambition* in the mind of a champion must be self-belief – or **confidence**. It has been my experience when meeting high-achievers in life and in sport that the one quality they share is that they genuinely believe that they are going to succeed. They have a confidence which goes beyond words, coming from a deep inner belief. Such high-achievers make themselves grounded and relaxed in the knowledge that they can win, and therefore when the pressure of victory looms they can cope with it.

Not all players have this confidence. The saddest sight in golf is to see a player who is approaching a Major victory break down and lose his swing because he cannot cope with the pressure. I can recall two separate occasions, in the Open and the Masters, when players who were in contention decided to play conservatively and use easy irons to make position. In both instances the players clearly did not believe they could win. Both shanked a simple iron shot. They lost their self-belief.

The third mental quality of a champion can be seen in the three golfers we have studied. Hogan, Jones and Hagen were all able to focus on the shot at hand and to be **in the present moment**. They managed to make their minds silent and remove any thoughts of what they had done previously, and they did not get ahead of themselves. Jones had to learn to accept the rub of the green and let it go. Hagen, on the other hand, knew that not every shot would have the outcome expected; when something bad happened, he dismissed it from his mind and got on with his game. Hogan had a mental image of a twenty-foot wall behind him, and while playing only thought of the next shot, never the previous one.

These three qualities of a champion's mindset have clear parallels in the *Silent Mind* approach to golf. A champion's *ambition* is similar to a golfer's **focus** when visualising the target. For the champion's *self-belief*, read **faith** in trusting the swing to deliver the intended stroke. And just as a champion is able to be *in the moment*, so a golfer can use **presence** to silence the mind and play a shot without conscious thought.

One player who epitomises all these qualities is Seve Ballesteros. We've already seen how ambitious Seve was, but in fact his self-belief went further than that: Ballesteros believed it was his destiny to be a great champion.

A rational mind would normally dismiss discussions of fate or destiny, but, looking at the success of Ballesteros, it appears that his belief in destiny made the difference. He believed he was destined to win – and therefore set out to do just that. Conversely, I am sure there are players who believe that they are not destined to win a Major tournament, and this becomes a mental block whenever they play in one.

When Ballesteros was a young rookie professional he met the golfer who was to become his hero, the South African, Gary Player. Ballesteros, who could be hot-blooded and emotional on the course, was astounded by Player's coolness and mental discipline. He came to admire Player's powers of concentration and strength of will, and tried to incorporate that into his own approach to the game.

In 1979, when he was 22, Ballesteros met Dr Alfonso Caycedo, who had studied transcendental meditation in India. Caycedo had created a new approach to modifying human consciousness which he called *sophrology*, the basic principle being to use meditation techniques to manage stress and bring harmony to the mind and body. He encouraged his pupils to use an exercise which involved visualising desired future outcomes. Ballesteros became convinced of the value of this technique, and became one of the first golf professionals to prepare himself mentally to confront pressure on the golf course.

When Ballesteros first met Caycedo he told him how he prepared to hit a shot. First he imagined it: he saw the shot and felt it in his mind. Caycedo told him that he was already practising sophrology intuitively. One of the first questions Caycedo asked Ballesteros was what in particular he wanted to achieve. Ballesteros' immediate answer was 'to win the Masters'.

As part of his Masters preparation, Ballesteros listened to meditation and visualisation tapes covering every aspect of the tournament. He became familiar in his mind with the sights, the sounds, the weather, the holes, the atmosphere, the tension and the crowds. Ballesteros says this was how he won his first Masters so easily. When he reached Augusta that year he expected to win.

Yet when the great moment of victory arrived, Seve didn't feel very emotional. This confused him. He had expected to be much more emotional about winning what he had always wanted. Caycedo later explained that in his visualisation exercises he had already experienced the emotion of winning. His mind could not experience it twice.

As he got older, Ballesteros' game became more erratic but his 'will to win' was as strong as ever. Even when past his prime he was still a force to be reckoned with in match-play. Like Hagen, his natural touch and sensational short game made him a tough competitor. 'My swing was all hands and brain,' he commented. 'Everything natural, my hands followed orders dictated by my brain.' This shows that he did not get in the way of his swing. He was a passionate and intuitive player, but he also understood the importance of allying a strong mind to a wonderful talent. Ballesteros trusted his ability to play the right shot and shape it as he needed to, whatever the situation.

What distinguishes a champion from an ordinary golfer? Simply, the champion knows how to get into the perfect mental state to hit the best possible shot.

I think of this in *Silent Mind* golf as the **Focus Faith Presence** approach.

Focus where the golfer sees the shot completed and the ball in the desired position.

Faith   where you trust yourself and your swing to deliver the stroke required.

Presence where, with no thoughts, you silence your mind just to 'be in the moment'.

If you can adopt the **Focus Faith Presence** approach in your golf game, I believe it will produce the single greatest change in your capacity to improve your form. It may not turn you into an Open champion, but I believe it will teach you how to think like a champion and to develop a champion's approach to your game.

'My mind is my biggest asset. I expect to win every tournament I play.'

Tiger Woods

SIX INCHES

In 1996, in preparation for a 72-mile endurance hike across Scotland, I was being trained by a former Special Forces sergeant. When I first met him he asked how far the distance was. With a degree of pride I said, 'Seventy-two miles.' 'No,' he replied, smiling and shaking his head. 'It's only six inches, the distance between your ears.' He told me that the physical selection process for his branch of Special Forces was the toughest in the British Army. He went on to explain that in this selection process it often wasn't the fittest candidate who made it through – it was the candidate who wanted it most. The candidate who could ignore the pain, the fatigue, the wind, the rain and just push themselves to keep going. He tapped his head just above his ear and said again, 'Six inches, the distance between your ears.'

Neither I nor anyone else can teach you the desire to win. I cannot convince you to do something you do not want to do. But what I can do is teach you something about the techniques you can use to improve your approach to the game. From my experience in different walks of life and my study of the great golfers of the game I have learned what is common is their attitude and expectations. I believe if you use these techniques you will be more successful.

Henry Ford, the founder of the Ford automobile company, summed it up perfectly when he said, 'If you think you can or think you can't you are usually right.'

> **'No matter what happens – never give up a hole . . . In tossing in your cards after a bad beginning you also undermine your whole game, because to quit between tee and green is more habit-forming than drinking a highball before breakfast.'**
>
> Sam Snead

SCIENTIAM IN ACTIONEM VERTENS

(TURNING KNOWLEDGE INTO ACTION)

MORE ON FOCUS

We shall now look at a selection of exercises you can practise to improve the quality of **focus** in your game.

In these pages I have described **focus** as the ability to pick a target and then leave the brain to lock onto it. This allows the subconscious mind to make the calculations required for the shot at hand.

One problem I encountered with students in the early days was that, when they thought they were focusing before the shot, they were really thinking, 'Anywhere on the fairway,' and not visualising a precise outcome. It is like saying, 'I want to be rich,' but not being specific about how you will create your wealth. **You need to have a focus on every shot.**

Curiously, most of us do have focus when it comes to putting. Before we putt, we pick up a point relative to the hole, right or left, where we think we need to aim, and then we attempt to get the pace just right.

So, the first exercise to help you develop a keen sense of focus in your subconscious mind is a putting exercise.

PUTTING ▶

(time: 30 minutes)

1. Go to a practice green with three balls in your pocket.
2. Stand three feet away from the hole. Address an imaginary ball that you have aligned with the hole.
3. Turn your head to look only at the hole and make five or six practice strokes, each time imagining the ball running into the hole.
4. Position a real ball in the place of your imaginary ball. Make three putts.
5. When you have sunk five putts in a row move to a new hole and repeat.

The purpose behind this exercise is to allow your imagination to visualise the shot you want to hit in advance of actually doing it. By looking only at the hole you create a target and focus point for yourself. By practising without looking at the club-head, you allow your subconscious mind and muscle memory to create what it believes is the correct swing for the putt.

DISTANCE PUTTING ▶

(time: 20 minutes)

1. Stand 20 feet away from the hole. Address an imaginary ball that you have aligned with the hole.
2. Turn your head to look only at the hole and make five or six practice strokes, each time imagining the ball running to within two feet of the hole.
3. Position a real ball in the place of your imaginary ball. Make three putts.
4. When you have put three putts in a row to within two feet, go to a new hole and try a longer or shorter putt.

The purpose behind this exercise is to let your imagination get a feel for the pace required. You should make five or six practice swings, instinctively. However, when the ball is placed in front of the club-head, it is natural to want to control the swing once again (and so tense up). This is why you must only hit the ball after five or six practice swings, and then strike the ball with confidence in exactly the same way as the practice swing.

It helps to do this exercise on the practice putting green before you go out and play a round of golf. It encourages you to trust your putting stroke more completely and helps you develop confidence in your swing, which is the cornerstone of the second aspect of *Silent Mind* – **faith**.

One of the main ways we inhibit our ability to execute a good shot is through performance anxiety. Frequently while on the course we will make a couple of perfect practice swings, and then execute a truly hideous shot that bears no resemblance to our previous textbook rehearsal. Why? What happened?

I believe this is because subconsciously we know the practice swing has no possible bad outcome – I don't know anyone who gets nervous taking a practice swing. But once we address the ball the swing is going to count towards our score and the outcome of the match.

By learning to trust our swing and keeping our mind completely silent and free from all thought, we enable ourselves to swing the club as perfectly as we would during a practice swing.

I BELIEVE

By **faith,** I mean having complete confidence in yourself and trusting your ability to execute the shot you are about to play. Some golfers distinguish themselves from others by their ability to improvise and shape the ball when they are up against a difficult shot, rather than their consistency of play from tee to green. That requires great imagination and technical excellence.

To do this, they change their swing subtly. More importantly, though, they believe that they can execute the shot. The club we most often associate with this type of wizardry is a pitching-wedge. When we think of players such as Seve Ballesteros, Phil Mickelson and Tiger Woods, it is their recovery shots around the green that we remember, rather than the many perfectly normal shots we see them hit in the course of a tournament. These players have the ability to see the shot in their mind's eye before they execute it. All players have the ability to imagine, but few players are able to eliminate self-doubt and translate what they imagine into reality.

Until you can see the shot and focus on what you see, your brain cannot plot the swing you require to execute it. If you cannot approach your swing with confidence, you will spend the rest of your life playing hit-and-hope. The following exercise is about seeing a variety of shots from the same lie with the same club.

PITCHING ▶

(time: one hour – yep, that's right, 60 minutes)

1. Take a sand-wedge and a dozen balls. Drop the balls at least 20 yards from the putting surface. Then pick an area on the green where you want the ball to finish.

2. Now imagine hitting a high lob shot with the sand-wedge and visualise the ball coming to rest in the spot you want it to finish.

3. Take six practice swings for the lob shot and then hit six actual shots at the target. Don't concern yourself with the outcome at this stage.

4. Using the same club from exactly the same spot, imagine playing a bump and run shot with the same club. This exercise is about imagination and execution, so even though this is not a club you would normally use from 20 yards off the green for a bump and run, I want you to use it on this occasion.

5. Again take six practice swings. Again hit six actual shots at the target.

6. Repeat this exercise a number of times until you are consistently hitting the majority of high lobs and bump and runs just as you have imagined them.

This exercise is about developing confidence in your swing and faith that you can execute the shots you are imagining. Too often we can imagine the shot but do not really believe we can execute it, which is why **it is so important that you completely believe that you can execute the shot**. Remember: **there is a world of difference between saying something and truly believing it**. While believing that something is going to happen does not guarantee that you will hit the perfect shot, it does greatly increase the likelihood that you will.

DRIVING

A well-swung drive off the first tee that finds the middle of the fairway feels great. It settles the nerves of every golfer regardless of handicap or experience. I have read accounts of world-class professionals, with many years of experience and success behind them, battling to control their nerves as they step onto the first tee for their opening drive. At a Major, butterflies appear in the stomach, palms turn sweaty and mouths go dry on that long walk to the first tee. This seems even more the case at the Ryder Cup, with many players finding the opening tee shot the most nerve-wracking shot of their careers.

The opening drive sets the tone for many of us. We have a long time to think about it, from the moment we wake, even if we are not consciously thinking of it. We are aware that it is a shot we have played many times before – and not always with a happy ending. It is the only shot of the round we have hours, instead of minutes, to think about.

The following exercise is been designed specifically to help us with our opening drive. This is a visualisation exercise which can be done at home or in the office during a break.

THE PERFECT SWING ▶

(time: five minutes)

Sit in an upright chair with both your feet on the ground. Your hands may be resting on your lap, or on the armrests. Back upright, eyes closed, breathing gently.

Visualise yourself making a perfect swing. I want you to see yourself as an image on a television screen making a perfect swing.

At the top of the back-swing, freeze the position. See yourself as if through a camera moving 360 degrees, examining that position from different angles. Admire the position you have at the top of the back-swing:

- eye on the ball
- shoulders turned
- club parallel to target line
- perfect balance.

Now visualise yourself in slow motion, executing a perfect downswing and making perfect contact with the ball. See the ball taking off down the perfect line, and see yourself maintaining perfect balance, keeping your head down, extending through the hitting area, getting your weight on to the left side and finishing your swing in the perfect follow-through position. Now freeze that position.

This exercise should last no more than five minutes, and can be repeated regularly to embed the image of the perfect swing and a good follow-through position.

Some people have difficulty with visualisation exercises. They find it hard to visualise what they are trying to imagine. If this applies to you, don't worry. If you cannot visualise, then try instead to create a good sense of emotion to accompany the shot, and embed that feeling in your subconscious mind.

You will find the more you do it, the easier the process gets. When I began visualising I could 'see' nothing. But over time, I've become able to visualise quite clearly and see myself as if on television.

This is not a frivolous exercise that finds its origins in new-age mumbo jumbo or some form of self-hypnosis. It is based on the simple principle that we perform in accordance with our level of expectation, and this expectation is normally based on past experience. **If we consistently visualise a perfect swing and put that clear image into our subconscious mind, then it becomes our expectation as it becomes our dominant image**. When it comes to playing a shot on the course, the subconscious mind will use that image to help muscle memory execute the swing we have imagined.

The main benefit of this exercise is that it creates a perfect image for the subconscious mind to use as a template for our muscle memory.

As I have mentioned before and will mention again (and again), imagination is no substitute for practice, which is why the *Silent Mind* mental conditioning program should be used as a tool to enhance coaching and professional instruction. Our muscle memory is developed through repetition, not simply imagination.

I would strongly recommend using this exercise before you practise and before you play a round of golf. The more proficient you become at this, the easier you will find it. You will be able to take it onto the course with you to such an extent that prior to hitting any shot you'll be able to close your eyes and visualise the shot in its fullness. In a matter of seconds you will be in a more balanced state of physical and mental preparedness.

> 'It is like a colour movie. First I see the ball where I want it to finish. Then the scene quickly changes and I see the ball going there. Then there is a sort of fade-out and the next scene shows me making the kind of swing that will turn the previous images into reality.'
>
> Jack Nicklaus on his pre-shot routine, 1992

GETTING RID OF THE INTERNAL GREMLINS

Before we hit an important shot **it is natural to experience moments of self-doubt.** It is natural to experience self-doubt and performance anxiety. If we didn't we would be robots. But such doubts rarely help us execute our intended shots. By contrast, when people attain a state of focus which enables perfect execution, sometimes called being 'in the zone', they describe this state with words like *calm*, *focus*, *timelessness*, *relaxation* and even *destiny*. They are free from fear and anxiety.

This heightened state of being 'in the zone' remains something of a mystery. People cannot enter the 'zone' at will. Players talk of it in the same hushed tones as the alchemists who tried to turn lead into gold. I have experienced it a number of times in my life, and have read accounts of athletes who have described exactly the same emotional sense: a knowledge and a certainty that all would be well, that they knew they were going produce the perfect shot.

I wonder what percentage of golfers give themselves negative feedback and focus on their bad shots, continuing to recall them throughout the round, compared with golfers who give themselves positive feedback, focusing on the good shots? I don't have any exact figures, but I'm sure it's heavily weighed towards the negative, with very few having positive thoughts. I base this on hundreds of conversations over the last twenty years with golfers who continue to beat themselves up over bad shots. They not only expect to hit a bad shot, but even use the shot as a validation of their being right (i.e. negative) in the first place.

What we endeavour to do in *Silent Mind* is to minimise the impact of these thoughts and feelings prior to hitting a shot.

I know people who play great golf on the practice ground when their pro or coach is watching, but when on the course, especially in competition, hit poor shot after poor shot and suddenly lose all confidence in themselves. Equally, I know the golfers who never practise and probably play fewer than 10 times a year, but who are naturally positive and competitive people with the ability to focus on every shot in any condition, giving themselves the best chance to maximise their skill.

Golf is very much a game of energy and flow, positive and negative. We experience it during match-play events at the club level. One missed short putt, a mis-hit iron, or a long putt holed by your opponent can change the whole course of the match. When the belief and confidence of one player improves, the advantage goes to them and the energy and momentum of the match will usually reflect this. However, if we can lock our emotional state, concentrate completely on the present moment and 'be here now', we will be in the best condition to enter the 'zone', free from negative thoughts and attachment to outcomes.

Though it may sound simple enough in theory, this will, in fact, be impossible if we have any negative thoughts chattering away in our head – those negative feelings and thoughts about losing. I have experienced being five-up in a match after nine holes, only to lose, and I am sure all golfers have memories of their own collapse on the course. In my disastrous match, the collapse began when my opponent said, 'I think you've got this wrapped up,' and I replied, 'I could still lose.' I then started over-thinking and over-trying. In contrast, I have also been four-down with five to play and told myself that I was going to win – and then won. The self-belief translated into confidence, which strengthened my ability to execute good shots under pressure, which swung the energy and momentum of the match to me, and away from my opponent.

> **'If you think positively and keep your mind on what's right, it gives you a better attitude. If you moan and groan and are disgusted, you play miserably too.'**
>
> Bernhard Langer

BEING IN THE MOMENT

The art of being wholly present in the moment, with no thoughts distracting you, no memories of past failures gnawing at your confidence and no imagined bad outcomes playing in your head, is the ideal state of mind on the golf course.

Being 'in the moment' is a state of complete freedom or timelessness. Time stands still, so that there is no sense of past or future, just a keen sense of *now*. We experience such moments throughout our lives. They usually involve strong emotional associations, such as when we fall in love, or witness the birth of our child – or watch our team finally win the championship. But these moments are not always positive experiences: the sensation also occurs in moments of distress, such as suffering a near-fatal accident (with the sensation of time slowing down), or being told we have cancer, or losing a loved one, or suffering any other emotionally traumatic experience.

These experiences become deeply and emotionally embedded in our subconscious minds because of their associated emotional delight or pain. In those moments of joy and fear, the sense of timelessness gives us insight and an understanding of being present in the moment. This is a key principal of the *Silent Mind* approach to golf.

Though most people can accept the notion of being in the present moment, they find it almost impossible to achieve. Why is this?

Few of these examples are planned for, and, as a consequence, this timeless state arises involuntarily, as the overload of emotional input heightens our sense of being alive in the present. The most common emotional responses are shock, joy, anger, fear and love. What we must *learn* is how to enter this timeless state *deliberately* as we stand over the golf ball, without any associated emotion – simply to clear our minds of all thought and let time stand still. To maximise our ability to play our best golf, we need our emotional state to be neutral. We need to suspend our emotions. Because if we don't control them they will control us, affecting the way we think and subsequently act.

I believe **the most common cause of choking in sport is imagining a negative outcome – defeat**. This outcome becomes so vivid that the associated emotion manifests itself as shortness of breath, dry mouth, clammy hands – the classic fight-or-flight adrenaline reflex that we have all experienced. This gets in the way of muscle memory, as we begin to try to *control* our swing, while battling strong negative emotions.

The cruel irony is that when we hit a bad shot – having previously imagined that we were going to do so – not only do we believe we were right to be afraid (given the outcome), we also fail to acknowledge that our negative thinking massively increased the probability of a bad shot in the first place.

So what is it we are afraid of?

Simple: the fear of failure.

When Boris Becker won the Wimbledon Men's Singles final at the age of 17, and then again at 18, he was rightly hailed as a tennis prodigy, and great things were expected of him. When he came back to attempt a third consecutive win, he was knocked out in the second round. At the press conference, journalists asked about the terrible disappointment of failing so early in the competition. Becker showed maturity in excess of his years as he put things into perspective. He said, 'Nobody died . . . I just lost a match.' Certainly it was in an important tournament, but ultimately it was just one match. Becker didn't beat himself up, or identify himself as being a failure. He was able to put the loss into perspective and continue with his life.

If we learn to accept failure as a possible outcome, albeit one we would prefer not to experience, we take much of the pressure off ourselves.

In 1970, Doug Sanders had a three-foot putt to win the Open championship at St Andrews in Scotland, a scenario every professional golfer dreams about. As he stood over the ball to make his putt, he suddenly stepped back and brushed away what many considered to be an imaginary blade of grass. He then settled himself back over the putt. He seemed to rush the putt and missed it, and suddenly a life-defining Major championship – only one moment earlier so very tantalisingly close – was now gone forever. What happened? It appears he got ahead of himself. In an interview he gave years later he said, 'As I looked at the second putt I was thinking about what I was going to do – throw the club in the air and bow to the gallery, and try to be a humble winner.' The following day, although he played very well, he lost an 18-hole play-off with Jack Nicklaus.

In another interview, some 30 years later, he was asked how often he thought about that putt. With self-effacing good humour, Doug Sanders replied, 'Some days I can go twenty minutes without thinking about it.' What impact did that miss, and his continued memory of it, have on the rest of his career? We will never know, but we can imagine. He was a wonderful golfer, but one cannot help but think that his self-confidence took a blow from which it never fully recovered.

To be free to play our best golf, and also to live our best life, **we must accept the reality and possibility of failure but – *crucially* – not identify ourselves with it.** Instead, we need to learn from it and understand it even though we may feel disappointed. There will be other opportunities in the future where we can, and will, succeed.

In golf therefore, difficult as it may seem at times, when our whole world seems to be falling apart and we are choking like an asthmatic in a feather factory, we must not lose confidence. We must not think about or be afraid of a negative outcome. We must focus on the next shot. We must consciously relax (the breathing exercise) then go through the mental pre-shot drill: **focus**, **faith** and **presence**.

The more we can relax, the more we free our mind and body, and the more we maximise our chances of hitting the perfect shot.

MASTERING THE PRESSURE PUTT ▶

(time: five to ten minutes)

The pressure putt will often induce tension due to a natural desire to make the putt, but our experiencing a stronger emotional response to missing the putt. The negative emotion, being more powerful, will cause us to worry, inducing self-doubt, and in some cases get the adrenaline surge that causes butterflies in the stomach, and in severe cases physical tremors.

This exercise is fantasy based, but builds up your confidence, and gives you a coping mechanism when facing a pressure putt.

1. Sit down in a chair and relax with both feet on the ground, slightly apart. Rest your hands gently in your lap.

2. Visualise yourself on the 18th green in an important match with a must-make four-foot putt to win the event for your team. Spend a few minutes listening to the *Silent Mind* CD (track 3), breathing in deeply and slowly and physically relaxing.

3. See the ball lying four feet from the hole. Become aware of the whole scene around you, the background noise, your opponent, your team mates standing by the green.

4. Now step into your body, and feel the nervous energy in your body. Feel the desire to win, the desire to make a good putt, all the time being aware of the tension in your body.

5. Walk up to the putt and as you do so, take a deep breath. Slowly inhale as you say to yourself, 'I am breathing in calm.' As you exhale, say to yourself, 'I am breathing out tension.'

6. Take a second deep breath. Slowly inhale as you say to yourself, 'I am breathing in confidence.' As you exhale, say to yourself, 'I am breathing out self doubt.'

7. When you take your third and final deep breath in and out see yourself settling over the putt, feeling totally relaxed, and making a perfect putt into the dead centre of the cup.

8. When you have done this, take a few deep breaths and slowly open your eyes, to finish the exercise, feeling relaxed and positive.

> **MASTERING THE PRESSURE PUTT** *(continued)* ▶
>
> The purpose of this exercise is to equip yourself with a pre-putt routine expressly designed for occasions when tension or fear threatens to interfere with the stroke or your concentration. This is an exercise I strongly recommend you do daily.

WHAT TO DO WHEN IT REALLY ALL GOES TO TRASH

You will be familiar with the golfing expression 'the wheels are coming off'. Golfers use it when they feel their swing start to deteriorate in the middle of a round: when they recognise that a period of bad play is beginning and that there is nothing they can do to prevent it.

I played in a four-ball better-ball knockout competition some years ago and began with a truly awful drive. I must have looked like a person swinging an axe in a lumberjack competition. I swung at the ball as though I thought at any moment it was going to jump off the tee and run for cover. The ball took off at a 45-degree angle, then started to slice, before diving into some penal rough. There was a somewhat prolonged pause, as there was nothing the other three players could say – other than to pretend it hadn't happened, which they didn't. So I hit a provisional – to the same place, of course – before giving my partner that well worn, universally acknowledged facial expression which means, 'Can you believe that?' Unfortunately for me, he could.

It would be great if I could say that I then started playing the best golf of my life, but I didn't. That opening drive was probably the best swing I put on the ball for the next five holes. By the time we got to the sixth tee, I was seriously considering giving up golf. My partner had played well and was entirely responsible for getting us two-up in the match.

On the walk to the sixth tee I gave myself a pep talk. I reminded myself I had played a lot of good golf in the past, and all I had to do was swing the club and stop trying to hit the ball so hard; just get back to the basics. In effect what I did – and have done ever since – is to hit the stop button that prevents me from having negative thoughts. I stopped beating myself up and I stopped worrying too much about the outcome of the match. Instead I reminded myself that I play golf because I enjoy it. That enforced mindset created an immediate change in attitude and encouraged me to stop over-thinking and to relax. So I'd like to give you the following advice: **should you find yourself having a day when your golf swing deserts you, give yourself an immediate attitude-check, and relax.**

Try to find some positive words that you like. My words are **love, joy** and **positive attitude**. They become a simple mantra to me, and help remove tension, and remind me that I play golf because I love it and want to play it joyfully. I also want a positive attitude at all times and in all situations. When I feel anxiety or a build up of tension come into my swing, I very slightly and deliberately slow down my walk, I breathe more consciously, and I repeat these very simple words to myself:

'Love, joy and a positive attitude.'

The immediate effect is to distract me completely from my negative mood and give me an appreciation of where I am and what I am doing. As I walk up to the ball before the shot I have a feeling of everything going into slow motion. My actions slow down, my breathing slows down and I quieten my racing mind.

We can choose to be positive or negative, because our attitude is at all times entirely under our control.

PANIC/CHOKE MANAGEMENT ▶

(time: five to ten minutes)

When we lose our form on a golf course, or lose three holes in a row in match-play, a feeling that our game is going into meltdown overwhelms us. We lose confidence and start over-thinking every aspect of our game. We do the precise opposite of what is required: we lose focus and faith and get so far ahead of ourselves that we are no longer 'being in the moment'.

This exercise is simple to do and is intended to neutralise your panic/stress reflex on the course.

1. Sit down in a chair and relax, with both feet on the ground, slightly apart. Rest your hands gently in your lap, and spend a few minutes listening to the *Silent Mind* CD (track 3), breathing in deeply and slowly and physically relaxing.

2. Visualise yourself feeling the gentle despair of playing badly having lost form. Feel the match slipping away from you. Feel your anger, frustration, your loss of confidence. (Though this is an unsettling and uncomfortable feeling, you need to experience it for the exercise to work.)

3. While aware of this feeling, take a deep, deliberate breath in and, as you breathe out, say to yourself, 'Relax.'

4. Continue to breathe in and out slowly and deeply, while saying, 'Relax,' until the negative mental and physical feelings are gone.

5. When the feelings have subsided, repeat to yourself: 'Focus, Faith, Presence.' Repeat it like a mantra, slowly and quietly. As you do so, feel yourself becoming ready to focus and more confident in yourself, and being aware only of the present moment.

6. When you have done this to your satisfaction, take a few deep breaths and slowly open your eyes to finish the exercise. Be sure you feel relaxed and positive.

The purpose of this exercise is to give you a routine to employ should you feel yourself becoming panicky or anxious or tensing up, especially during a patch of bad play.

'It was just one of those days. I had the feeling that no matter what the distance might be on the greens, I had the line right and I had nothing but good positive thoughts. I can understand better now how the great players manage to keep their game going on a high.'

Rodger Davis

EXIT! EXIT!

Skydivers have a main and a reserve parachute. After they exit from the plane at 12,500 feet they deploy their main parachute at a pre-determined altitude (usually between 3000 and 4000 feet). Statistically, I have been informed that approximately one time in every 607 the main parachute will deploy with a malfunction, which means either it will not open, or it will open partially, but sufficiently distorted as to prevent a safe landing. Either way, the skydiver has an emergency on their hands and has to do something about it.

Every person who learns to skydive has drilled into them from their first day of training what to do when they have a malfunction: they initiate their emergency procedure in a precise order. They practise this on the ground, and sometimes even in the minutes before the pilot switches on the green light and shouts 'Exit! Exit!' skydivers go through their emergency procedures.

The procedure I learned was very straightforward: you look and locate your red cutaway handle, then hold it in your right hand.

You then look and locate your silver reserve handle, and hold it with your left hand. Then, you peel the red cutaway handle from the Velcro and punch it downwards; this detaches the main canopy from your harness. Pull and punch downwards with the reserve handle; this deploys the reserve parachute. I soon realised that the emergency procedures are a matter of life and death. Knowing this, skydivers practise again and again and again and again. They drive these procedures into their subconscious mind so that **when the emergency happens, you don't think, you act.**

In golf, we have *mental* malfunctions. When we are on the golf course, and feel ourselves getting angry or upset, it can help to find those 'calm' words – the particular words that will quickly help us restore a positive attitude. You may choose something obvious, like 'peace', 'calm', 'relax', or 'chill'. You may choose other, entirely different words. The key is to find and use words that work for you, so that when you feel any mental malfunction begin, you can immediately go into your 'emergency drills' and, metaphorically, get your reserve parachute out. This will quickly return you to the perfect state for *Silent Mind* golf.

PRACTISE WITH PURPOSE

Very few club golfers practise with any real sense of purpose. Most of them, my former self included, go to the range, pull out their wedge (because that's what the pros do) and hit some shots to warm up. What we really need to do is start striking the ball consistently and make ourselves feel confident as we go to the first tee.

At my local commercial driving range, which is very busy most evenings, I see many people stand up and hit the ball as hard as they can, trying to hit the back fence at the 250-yard mark. These keen players at the range come in all ages and sizes. They hit one ball after another, rarely bothering to watch where it goes.

If you do not practise the mental conditioning techniques described in this book then it will be impossible to benefit from them on the golf course. You will remember parts of what I've talked about, and I'm sure you'll have some occasional success, but **for consistent results you need to put in consistent practice**. You will be familiar with the expression, 'What you put in is what you get out.' This is why I recommend allocating ten minutes out of *every day* to practising the mental conditioning exercises that come with the CD in this book.

'What? Ten minutes! Do you have any idea how busy I am?'

Sure, I know how busy you are. But ask yourself a question: how badly do you want to be the best player you can be? How much of each day are you willing to give up to become that player? Simply quit ten minutes a day of doing another pointless activity (which you were probably unaware you were doing anyway). If you can manage ten minutes every day, you will rapidly see improvements.

The improvements will be modest at first, as you gradually embed the visualisation and master 'silencing' the mind. However, slowly but surely, shots will follow on beautifully from practising mental conditioning. Remember: **the more you practise silencing the mind, the easier you'll find it.** And when you are able to do this on the course, you will find you trust your swing, and are able to strike those perfect shots.

When we learn consciously to 'get out of our own way', to stop thinking and let our subconscious mind operate through muscle memory, we then allow the mind to do what it does best: help us execute complex physical actions with ease.

VISUALISATION ▶

(time: ten minutes)

Our subconscious minds do not differentiate emotionally between the real and imagined. Therefore, if we imagine a very sad event, it will make us feel physically upset; the opposite is equally true.

This exercise is fantasy-based but used as a way of building up your confidence on the golf course.

1. Sit down in a chair and relax with both feet on the ground, slightly apart. Rest your hands gently in your lap.

2. Visualise yourself 200 yards from the green, playing a close game that you want to win. See yourself smiling, looking and feeling relaxed, with the knowledge that you are going to make a good swing and put the ball on the green.

3. Now, step into the scene, and observe yourself up close; see how calm, confident and relaxed you are, fully prepared to hit this perfect shot.

4. Now step into your body, and see and feel the scene from your own point of view – no longer an observer. Breathe deeply, taste the air, feel the club in your hand. Tell yourself you are feeling confident. Be aware of the lack of tension in yourself. Take a full but relaxed practice swing and look at the target on the green. Focus on the place you want the ball to come to rest.

5. Step up to the ball, and as you settle in and take position, look one more time at the target and say, 'Focus,' as you settle over the ball. Prior to initiating the swing, say quietly to yourself, 'Faith.'

6. When you are ready to swing, say, 'Presence.' (I use and recommend this as the trigger word, but if you wish you may use another word – or a small physical action if you prefer. This word or action becomes the initiator for the take-away of the swing.) Feel yourself making this perfectly balanced swing with great tempo, striking the ball, and rotating through to the perfect follow-through position. As you look up, you see your ball flying directly towards the target you have selected.

7. Repeat Steps 2 to 6 a number of times, until the image and scenario are clearly felt and experienced in your imagination.

VISUALISATION (continued) ▶

When you have done this, take a few deep breaths and slowly open your eyes, to finish the exercise.

The purpose of this exercise is not only to have you visualise; It also enables you to *feel*, subconsciously, your pre-shot routine. When you are on the course you will have a record of it in your subconscious mind. This is an exercise I strongly recommend you do daily, while using the CD that accompanies this book.

'I don't really like too much thinking. I like to have it clear and just go ahead and hit it. Sometimes I think if you think too much, you're thinking too many things.'

Sergio García

ACCEPTANCE

When a young child plays a game and loses, you will often find that this is immediately followed by a tantrum. The child refuses to accept they have lost and gets angry and cries. The sense of injustice is unbearable for many young children, and no amount of reasoning will console them.

As we get older and (hopefully) wiser, we learn to accept that losing is part of life. That it's not a matter of whether we win or lose, but how we deal with either or both of those outcomes. We need to **accept things as they are and not as we wish them to be**. This does not mean that you have to like losing or that losing does not matter.

It simply means that the only effect it has on us is the importance we attach to it.

We *will* make mistakes. It is one of the qualities that make us human. We will experience success and failure in life. Neither one is an end in itself but simply an experience to which we should not attach too much significance. We should enjoy success and learn from failure, accepting both as outcomes and not validations of who we are or how we feel about ourselves.

I have watched the most beautifully struck shots get the most hideously unfair bounce, and end up unplayable. Equally I have seen badly struck shots ricochet off a tree and end up six inches from the hole.

In golf there are only outcomes. It has never been a fair game – there are too many outside factors to manage. There are good outcomes and bad outcomes. The important thing, whatever the outcome, is to accept it. Do not immortalise the shot in your memory as a cruel blow of fate that you didn't deserve, and replay it endlessly in your mind. Once it has happened, forget it and move on. It's in the past, so get on with living in the present. We have all been the victim of an opponent's outrageous good fortune, and at other times we have been that lucky so-and-so ourselves. Accept the outcome, remember the good and forget the bad, then move on.

We are not perfect, much as we would like to be. Be willing to accept yourself as you are – it will free you in ways you cannot imagine. You will no longer need to make excuses, blame others, complain about circumstances or even apologise to your partner when you hit a lemon. Be confident in the knowledge that you tried your best. If you beat yourself up about your poor performance, ultimately, you will realise golf is a game you no longer enjoy.

Remember golf is a game to be played for fun. If you're not having fun, something's wrong, and it is up to you to fix it.

Acceptance does not mean giving up. It does not mean we give up believing we can improve or win. **Acceptance means that, whatever happens, we acknowledge it, accept it and move on.**

Sadly, very few golfers do this.

LETTING GO OF BAD SHOTS ▶

(time: five to ten minutes)

There are few exercises in golf more fruitless than replaying a bad shot over and over in your mind after you have played it. It serves no purpose, other then to reinforce a negative memory and associated emotion. Yet for some people this becomes a ruminating thought that stays with them for the next few hours, or in some sad cases an entire lifetime.

This exercise is simple and is designed to stop you replaying the bad shot, irrespective of how painful or significant in terms of the outcome of the match it appears to be.

1. Sit down in a chair and relax with both feet on the ground, slightly apart. Rest your hands gently in your lap. Spend a few minutes listening to the *Silent Mind* CD (track 3), breathing in deeply and slowly, and physically relaxing.

2. Visualise yourself having hit your most destructive shot during a match with your biggest rival. Whatever that shot is, see the ball land, be fully aware of your negative response to it.

3. While aware of this feeling, take a deep, deliberate breath in and as you breath out smile gently and say something positive to yourself which will allow you to put it in perspective: 'It's not life or death'; 'It's only a game'; 'I've got the love of my friends and family, everything is fine.' (Choose words which have meaning to you and are positive.)

4. Continue to visualise yourself walking on from the shot just played. As you do so, feel the fresh air, feel the ground beneath your feet. Continue to say quietly to yourself whilst gently smiling, 'I love this game,' or another expression which sits comfortably with you.

LETTING GO OF BAD SHOTS *(continued)* ▶

5. Repeat to yourself: 'Focus, Faith, Presence.' Repeat it like a mantra, slowly and quietly, and as you do so feel yourself becoming ready to focus, becoming more confident in yourself, and being aware only of the present moment.

6. When you have done this to your satisfaction, take a few deep breaths and slowly open your eyes to finish the exercise. Be sure to feel relaxed and positive.

The purpose of this exercise is to give you a routine to think positive thoughts immediately after a bad shot and get your mind back into the present moment.

> **'You can't make it happen.
> You've got to let it happen.'**
>
> Ken Venturi

LOSING

I remember playing a singles match against a fellow who when off the course was great fun, but on the course he was a win-at-all-costs type. He identified himself as a winner and was very competitive. He also had a very good record in singles; no one ever really wanted to play him because they knew he was not going to crack under pressure. To make it worse, he was not a good winner. He wanted to beat you so badly that as soon as the match began he would do everything he could to win (including act as his own cheerleader and rules official). Once he had won, he showed very little class and afterwards, back in the bar, was only too keen to tell you that he had 'kicked your ass'.

It was part of who he was; he was boastful, but there was no malice in his heart.

I remember playing him one summer in an important singles match. After 17 holes we were all square. I needed half a point from my match to win the event for my team.

He hit a badly pulled three-iron from the tee. I hit mine down the middle. He then pushed a six-iron over the right-hand side of the green into a bunker. My shot was a full eight-iron but I didn't want to hit a full shot, so I took an easy seven and hit it straight at the pin. It drifted left. The pin was cut 12 feet from the left edge of the elevated green. The ball landed right on the cusp of the green, bounced the wrong way and ended up down against a tree.

My opponent played from the bunker and looked as though he would take five. I elected not to take a drop and ended up making six. We shook hands and retired to the bar. Once again he told the audience that he had kicked my ass, which tasted all the sweeter, I imagine, as his team won the competition as a result of his win against me.

After three days of competitive golf, the celebrations had calmed down somewhat and I said to him, 'Well, at least I hope I was a good loser.' What he said to me next is something I've never forgotten. He said, 'Show me a good loser, and I'll show you a loser.'

When I was a young man I hated losing, because, as I now realise, I allowed myself to identify with the experience and it became a manifestation of who I was. Many people do this and think if they lose they *are* losers. As a result I stopped competing. When I did compete, I put myself under such pressure that, win, lose or draw, I never enjoyed a single match. Given the choice of winning or losing, everyone would prefer to win. But if we make the losing such a big deal, such a genuinely painful experience, then we allow it to become a dominant thought. It quickly then becomes a self-sabotaging mechanism.

When you lose, accept the outcome. It's okay to be disappointed, even angry and upset, but only for ten seconds. Any longer and you're wasting valuable time in your life.

If you continue to relive bad shots over and over again, much like Doug Sanders after losing the Open, eventually this becomes a self-sabotaging ball and chain around your ankle. Failure now becomes your dominant expectation.

Over the years I've had the good fortune to meet and be influenced by many golfers who have a wonderful sense of balance in their attitude to the game. If you met them in the clubhouse afterwards you would not be able to tell if they had won or lost. They did not gloat in victory or become miserable in defeat. Curiously, more often than not, I believe they won because they reduced the pressure on themselves and freed themselves to play relaxed, confident golf.

I once played in a four-ball match with a pro who was a very good ex-tour player. We were roundly beaten five and four, by another player and pro pairing. Afterwards all my partner could talk about was how beautiful the course was, and how impressive the other professional had been.

CONNECT TO YOUR CONFIDENCE

There is a quote so well worn it has become a cliché. I have heard it attributed to many different characters, including artists and sporting characters, both living and dead. It is most often attributed to the golfer Gary Player, who responded to a comment about his luck by saying, 'The more I practise, the luckier I get!'

This is not only true for golf, it is true for life as well. In life, as in golf, everyone seems hell-bent on finding a quick fix to their problems, seeking a miracle cure, or a get-rich-quick scheme. You only have to watch some of the late-night infomercials on television to see the variety of aids (some good, some awful) that promise variations on the same thing: weight loss, physical fitness and, my personal favourite, the miracle golf aid.

Some work for the same reason that 'lucky charms' work for some people – simply because the person believes in them. If this seems doubtful, why do so many top golfers in the world have personal superstitions and lucky charms? They might have a specific number on their ball, or use the ball marker that they've used for decades. Why does Tiger Woods always wear a red shirt going into the final round of a tournament?

Anything that helps you feel mentally relaxed and gives you confidence is a good thing, and if you require a 'charm' or 'trigger' to fire up your confidence, by all means, use it. I doubt that Tiger Woods will start selling 'game improvement' red shirts: for him it's a personal thing. The important thing is to connect to your confidence. Find what works, and use it to your advantage.

'SEE IT'

It is vitally important to understand the impact of belief on outcome. It is one thing to say you believe, but if this belief is going to effect real change, then there is absolutely no room at all for scepticism – as in, 'I'll believe it when I see it.' It is one thing to say you believe something; it is altogether another thing to see it in your mind's eye and believe that it is a future reality.

How many Major champions do you think dreamt about winning a Major? How many of them, as a young professional, visualised one day holding the trophy of a Major championship in their arms? All of them. Even those winners who came from nowhere and posted a once-in-a-lifetime low score and, against the odds, won a Major. I believe they had already imagined and seen in their mind's eye – many times before – themselves as a Major championship winner.

> **'Every day I went down to the practice tee where they had a scoreboard with all the past Open champions' names on it and I stood there and visualised my name etched on the scoreboard.'**
>
> Gary Player on winning the 1965 US Open

DAILY MENTAL EXERCISE

The heart of *Silent Mind* golf is found in attaining the right mental state when we stand over the ball. The practice and preparation is not done on the course. When it comes to mental conditioning, the preparation is done off the course, then applied at will on the course

Daily mental conditioning through meditation is a powerful way to effect positive change in lowering your score and playing better golf.

This does not mean we should neglect practising our swing to make it mechanically better. I would encourage you to practise at least once a week. This may be on the putting green, at the short game area or at a driving range, but this one hour of actual practice will improve your muscle memory and other areas of your swing.

There is no 'secret', no technical gimmick. The more mental conditioning you do, the quicker you will condition your mind to create the perfect conditions to enter the 'zone' – and so to execute the best possible shot.

Good luck, enjoy, remember to breathe and play with love, joy and a positive attitude.

'When you're really on, a calmness comes over you.'

Mark O'Meara

THE GREATEST SHOT I EVER SAW

My father, according to family legend, was given a cut-down golf club on a family holiday as a young boy, and developed a lifelong love of the game. While studying medicine he played to a handicap of scratch, set the course record at his club and went on to win its club championship. He once played in the British Amateur Championship, which for a time-poor general practitioner in Glasgow was surely a testament to his ability.

When I was four years of age, my father introduced me to the game with my own cut-down wooden shafted club. By the time I was eight, I would regularly accompany him to the golf club on a Saturday and Sunday morning, where I would play with some other young players while he would take part in a match with friends. Occasionally, if I had no game of my own, my father would invite me to caddy for him, which in reality meant pulling his trolley.

Wisely, considering my age, he never asked me for any advice, yardage or opinion on his shots.

Although my father died far too early (over 33 years ago as I write this), there are certain aspects of his swing that I remember – his forward press of the hands and ever-so slight turn of the head to the right, that signalled the swing's take-away. I did not think of him as being a particularly special golfer, as he was simply my dad. What did I know about the complexity of the game? My father was a particularly good driver of the ball and he was usually the longest hitter in his group, straight down the fairway. Indeed, the comments of his partners I recall were always complimentary and reflect that aspect of his game.

Beyond these recollections, and the sense of being tired from pulling the trolley, I remember very little of those rounds. But there is one shot from those weekend morning matches that I will remember for the rest of my life.

Back in 1964 my father was a member of Erskine golf club, about 12 miles from Glasgow on the banks for the River Clyde. On this particular day, my father was playing much as normal, hitting his drives long and straight down the fairways. After playing the short par-three sixth hole we arrived at the seventh tee. Now, the seventh hole at Erskine is a long par-four, played from an elevated tee to a slightly uphill fairway that slopes from right to left. A good drive on this hole should land on the right side of the fairway to allow it to run down towards the middle – otherwise, it risks running into a strategically placed bunker, or light rough, making reaching the green in two very difficult.

When my father used his driver, he would tee his ball up much higher than other players. In fact, the whole ball appeared to be above the face of his driver, which I always thought a little unusual, as he had taught me to have half the ball showing above the driver clubface at address.

I have little recollection of the original drive. I imagine my father hit it long and straight up the right-hand side of the fairway. But as he picked up his tee, one of his companions commented that the length and flight of the drive was due to the fact my father teed the ball so high. My father replied that the height of the tee had nothing to do with the length of the shot.

It is what happened next that remains so vivid in my mind.

My father told his friends that he could tee it twice as high and still hit the same shot, since it was the strike and not the height of the ball off the ground that mattered. To which the same companion replied, 'Well, let's see you do it.'

Without a word being spoken, my father took out a second tee. He used to play with long plastic tees that were slightly hollow in the middle, which meant it was possible to put one inside the other to create a 'double-length' tee – which is what he now did. He then placed this in the ground and balanced a second ball on top – now a good one and a half inches above the top of his driver.

He took his driver in hand and prepared to hit the shot. We all watched intently as he stood behind the ball and stared up the fairway, longer than usual, took his position over the ball and settled himself to play the shot.

At that very moment, before my father drew the club back to take the shot, I knew with a certainty that I've rarely experienced in life that he was going to rip that drive up the right-hand side of the fairway. I had seen him miss short putts and thin a ball out of a bunker on several occasions, so I understood that bad shots happened. But on that Sunday morning on the seventh tee at Erskine golf club, with the ball teed up much higher than I'd ever seen before, and under the collective pressure of hitting an excellent drive, time stood still.

The ever-so slight forward press and fractional tilting of his head to the right triggered the start of his swing sequence. I watched the ball hiss through the air and begin its long, high climb away from the tee up into the sky towards the right-hand side of the fairway. It seemed to climb forever before falling to earth and coming to rest a few yards in front of his original drive.

Momentarily he looked at me and smiled, before lifting the tees from the ground and saying to the man who had challenged him, 'Tee height has nothing to do it.'

It remains the greatest shot that I have ever seen up close and live, and as I write this it I can still feel a tingle in my skin. I can see my father smiling at me as he picked up the tees, the red leather cover of the driver being put over the club, and the mustard coloured sweater with the moth-hole near the shoulder. Pride was at stake, no doubt about that. When he hit the shot he didn't turn to the others or do anything dramatic, he turned to me and smiled. He had hit that shot out of sight for his eight-year-old kid in short pants lugging his cart, who, like all young boys, believed his dad was a superman.

I have witnessed many extraordinary shots on the golf course and seen strokes of genius on television, but that shot more than any other remains for me a moment of transcendental magic. I recognise now that my father had the ability to focus on where he wanted that ball to land. I have no doubt he had faith that he could execute the shot. I don't know if he stilled his mind, but I believe on that day 45 years ago, for one brief moment, he entered the 'zone' and time stood still, as my father hit the greatest shot I ever saw.

ABOUT THE AUTHOR

Robin Sieger is a successful businessman, bestselling author, and broadcaster, with offices in the UK and the USA. Robin is a leading success strategist and is ranked as one of the top motivational speakers in the world.

At the age of 29, Robin was diagnosed with cancer. It was this life-changing experience that made him determine to re-examine his notion of success.

Robin is the author of four books including the international bestseller *Natural Born Winners*, which is sold in over 80 countries worldwide.

He has a world-class reputation as a conference speaker who passionately delivers high-impact presentations that are informative, inspiring and entertaining.

Robin's humour and ability to connect emotionally with audiences has seen him become the first-choice speaker at major conferences for some of the world's most successful companies, including, GM, HSBC, IBM, Coca Cola, Nokia and Microsoft, where he received the highest ranking of any external speaker.

He holds the world record for the coldest round of golf ever played, 18 holes at −26ºC in Fairbanks, Alaska on 22 December 2001.

For more information on *Silent Mind* golf instruction, offered by Robin Sieger, please visit *www.silentmindgolf.com* or send an e-mail to *info@silentmindgolf.com*.

Or you may write directly to *robin@silentmindgolf.com*.

Robin Sieger is based in Charlotte, North Carolina and Edinburgh, Scotland. He travels internationally delivering keynote motivational presentations to organisations, institutions and companies worldwide. His company, Sieger International, offers a wide range of seminars and educational programs on peak performance and success to both the public and private sector.

For more information about how to book Robin and Sieger International please visit *www.siegerinterntional.com*.

To enquire about Silent Mind golf instruction for corporate golf outings, private lessons or a keynote talk at a business event, please contact:

In the UK Sieger International Ltd
(toll free)
0845 2305400

In the USA Sieger International Inc.
(toll free)
877 743 4370